Creative
Doll
Makeovers

Creative Doll Makeovers

A STEP-BY-STEP GUIDE

Jan Tucker

Sterling Publishing Co., Inc.
New York

Prolific Impressions Production Staff:
Editor in Chief: Mickey Baskett
Copy Editor: Phyllis Mueller
Graphics: Dianne Miller, Karen Turpin
Photography: Jerry Mucklow, Steph's Studio
Administration: Jim Baskett

Library of Congress Cataloging-in-Publication Data

Tucker, Jan.
  Creative doll makeovers : a step-by-step guide / Jan Tucker.
      p. cm.
  Includes index.
  ISBN-13: 978-1-4027-2452-7
  ISBN-10: 1-4027-2452-7
1. Dollmaking.   I. Title.
TT175.T83 2006
745.592'2--dc22

                                                    2006007579

2 4 6 8 10 9 7 5 3 1

Published by Sterling Publishing Co., Inc.
387 Park Avenue South, New York, NY 10016
© 2007 by Prolific Impressions, Inc.
Distributed in Canada by Sterling Publishing
c/o Canadian Manda Group, 165 Dufferin Street,
Toronto, Ontario, Canada M6K 3H6
Distributed in the United Kingdom by GMC Distribution Services,
Castle Place, 166 High Street, Lewes, East Sussex, England BN7 1XU
Distributed in Australia by Capricorn Link (Australia) Pty. Ltd.
P.O. Box 704, Windsor, NSW 2756, Australia

Sterling ISBN-13: 978-1-4027-2452-7
ISBN-10: 4027-2452-7

For information about custom editions, special sales, premium and corporate purchases, please contact Sterling Special Sales Department at 800-805-5489 or specialsales@sterlingpub.com.

About the author

Jan Tucker

Jan D. Fougner Tucker has worked in the design field most of her life, for twelve years as Department Coordinator and Instructor of interior design at the University of North Dakota – Williston and later in commercial design in Minot, North Dakota. In 1999, she opened her business, Professional Business Interiors, in Minot, ND.

The second of John and Peggy Bearce Fougner's five children, Jan was born in Williston, North Dakota. She attended Williston public schools and graduated from Williston High School in 1972. In college she studied interior design, earning an A.A.S. degree, and she holds a B.S. degree in education.

Her four children (including twin boys) have always been the center of her life. In 2000, she re-located to Nebraska and gained two step-daughters after she married her husband on the Roseman Covered Bridge in Winterset, Madison County, Iowa.

While in Nebraska, Jan became fascinated with the art of "reborn" dolls. After much research and conversation with other doll makers, Jan began creating "reborn" dolls of her own. It is thrilling to see how much joy one of these dolls brings. Jan loves to take her dolls to hospitals and nursing homes for patients to enjoy.

Jan now resides in Kansas City, MO, where she is making plans to resume her commercial design career.

A Note from Jan,
I wish to thank all the "reborn" doll makers out there who inspired my doll making and helped me discover many of my techniques. There are many sites on the internet where you can view other "reborn" dolls, buy supplies for doll making, and learn a lot about doll making techniques. You can search for "reborn" and gain a list of numerous sites to visit.

Table of Contents

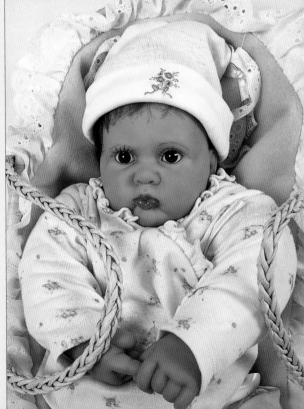

Introduction

Create a Lifelike Doll to Love

The doll makeover process involves taking a vinyl play doll and, through the application of color and various additions, transforming it to create a realistic-looking doll for display purposes. The completed doll is a work of art, and it often resembles a real baby. It may remind the artist of her own child, a niece or nephew, or a grandchild. This is an interesting aspect of the doll makeover art form – the possibility of creating a doll that captures for display a particular stage in a loved one's development.

My interest in doll makeovers was sparked by some "reborn" dolls I discovered while browsing online. The term was new to me, and the dolls were so realistic that I expected them to start breathing and moving. After that initiation, I visited a number of doll artists' web sites and read about the methods they used. When I felt I'd gathered enough information about the doll makeovers, I decided to try it. I have learned much from working on dolls for the last several years and feel it is time to share this art with others.

This book describes and shows you the steps I use to create a doll, from preparing the base doll, to coloring, adding eyes and hair, and making various types of cloth bodies and accessories. You'll also see numerous examples of my finished dolls as well as the work of other doll artists. At the end of the book, you'll find patterns for making cloth bodies for dolls of many shapes and sizes.

This hobby is fun and creative, but doll makeovers require a commitment of time (about three to four weeks) and money (for the tools and supplies). You'll also need to set aside a place in your home where you can work on dolls and store your supplies. It's

up to you, the artist, to decide which methods work best for you. As you work, you will develop your own style and create a doll that reflects your personal taste. I encourage you to learn the skills and develop your own methods so your finished dolls are an expression of you.

I treat each doll as a blank canvas and turn it into my personal masterpiece. As I continue to explore this creative outlet, I find I keep learning and inventing new techniques for applying color to the vinyl, rooting hair, or just making the final result better. Creating realistic-looking doll babies is a great hobby. Express yourself, and take your time. I hope you enjoy it as much as I do!

Before and after: The naked doll pictured at right is the same type of base doll that was used to create the charming doll makeover, pictured at left. For more on this doll, see "Jacy Bryn" in the section titled Jan's Nursery.

Supplies

The supplies you will need are wide and varied. Some of the items you can find in your own home. Start at a toy store or a discount department store for your base doll. Other supplies can be found at craft shops or departments. Some specialty doll making items can be found at shops where doll making supplies are sold or found on the internet.

Dolls

Your doll makeover begins with a play doll made of soft vinyl. It can be a full-body vinyl doll or a doll with a cloth body and partial vinyl limbs. Dolls with silicone bodies can be used, but they are usually much more expensive.

Your doll makeover will include removing the doll's original color from the vinyl and recoloring the vinyl for a more lifelike appearance. You'll also construct a soft cloth torso or replace the doll's cloth body with an improved cloth body and add new hair, eyelashes, eyebrows, and eyes.

You can find these dolls at toy stores and discount department stores, or you can shop online – doll manufacturer's websites have charts that show the dolls' faces. Another option is to recycle a used vinyl doll. I recommend starting with a less expensive base doll

for your first doll makeover because you can (and likely will) make mistakes as you learn.

When choosing a doll, look for one that attracts your attention, one whose facial features and expression pleases you. There are many nice lifelike faces available. If you intend for your doll to resemble a particular baby (this is called "portraiting"), shop for a doll that looks similar to that baby.

Another consideration is the size of the doll – they come in a variety of sizes from 8" tall, a 19"–21" newborn size, and on up to over 22" for toddler size. When you choose the size of the doll, then you'll be able to select eyes of the appropriate size and decide what patterns to use for making the body. Take your time, and have fun while looking.

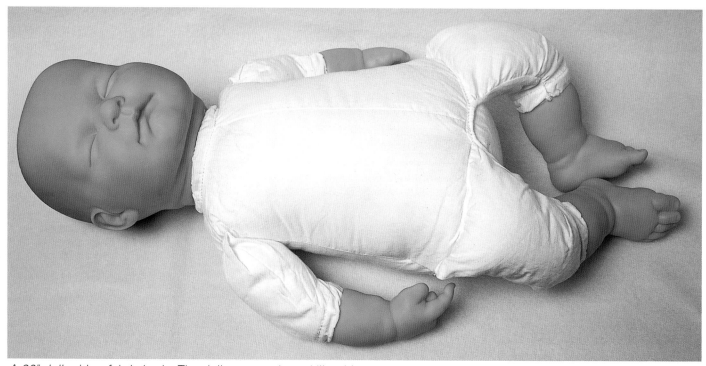

A 20" doll with a fabric body. The doll was purchased like this.

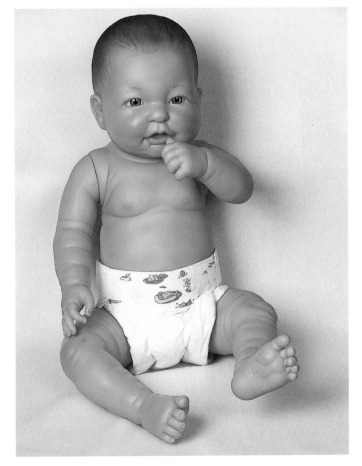

Pictured above: Three 14" all-vinyl dolls that are available as toys. Note the differences in their faces and their shapes.

Pictured left: 22" all-vinyl doll as purchased.

Doll Body Supplies

These are the miscellaneous supplies you'll use for cleaning your doll prior to applying the new coloring and for constructing and assembling your doll's new body.

Paint Remover

A multi-purpose paint and adhesive remover is needed for removing factory coloring. This product will remove the color but won't damage the vinyl. It is available in the paint section of hardware stores and home improvement centers. You can also use acetone to remove the coloring.

Fabric

The doll's body or torso will be made from soft cloth. Choose **flannel or doeskin** for the outside of the body. Fabric, the color of the doll's skin is preferable; but white can be used.

You will need **tightly woven fabric** such as **cotton** for the weight bags.

Choose **non-woven fusible interfacing** for reinforcing some areas of the body.

A small piece of black felt is used for backing the doll's nostrils.

Filler

Polyester stuffing is used for stuffing the doll's soft body.

Plastic pellets (a 2 lb. bag) is needed for filling weight bags for the body and head. Adding weight bags gives your doll a realistic feel. *Option:* Use sterilized sand instead. To sterilize sand, place in an oven-safe container and bake at 350 degrees for one hour.

Plastic Cable Ties

The vinyl head and limbs are attached to the cloth body with plastic cable ties. You may need small and large sizes, depending upon the size of your doll. The ties are the kind used to bundle telephone and computer cables. You will need them in two sizes – an 8" small size and a 14" large size.

Plastic Doll Joints

These can be found where doll making supplies are sold. They are used for making dolls with jointed arms and legs. See the section on Making Bodies for more information.

Adhesives

- **Clear silicone sealer** is needed for sealing the ends of partial limbs and sealing rooted hair inside the head.
- **White craft glue**, such as a "tacky" glue, attaches wigs and eyelashes to the vinyl head.

Applicators

Cotton swabs and cotton balls, to use for removing and applying coloring and mixing oil paints.

Clothing

You can choose clothing for your doll before you start your doll makeover and create a doll for a specific outfit, or you can choose the clothing for the doll after the doll is finished. You can see just some of the clothing options and get ideas for dressing your doll by looking at the photographs in the sections titled Jan's Nursery and Gallery of Dolls.

Optional Accessories

You can accessorize your doll and pose him or her with toys like stuffed animals and dolls and doll- or child-size furniture. You also can make accessories for your doll like pacifiers (they're held in place with magnets) and baby bottles (complete with faux formula). For lists of supplies and complete instructions, see "Making Magnetic Pacifiers" and "Making Baby Bottles."

Pictured left to right: Multi-purpose paint and adhesive remover, cotton balls, black felt scrap, cable ties, clear silicone sealer, plastic pellets (shown in the package and in a plastic container), scissors

Tools

These are the basic tools you'll need to get started with your doll makeover.

Scissors

Scissors for cutting fabric are needed for making the cloth bodies. You will also need a pair of all purpose scissors. Always keep your fabric cutting scissors for just that purpose or they will dull easily and will not work well for cutting fabric.

Drilling Tools

- **A regular drill and small drill bit (1/16" size)** is needed for drilling the nose pilot holes.
- **Multi-purpose electric hand tool**, such as a Dremel® tool, with a routing bit is used for enlarging the nose openings and a sanding bit for removing hair lines from the head.

Pliers

Use **Needlenose pliers** for tightening cable ties and cutting off the ends of sewing machine needles for rooting hair.

Cutting Tools

- **Wire cutters or snippers** come in handy for a multitude of tasks – such as trimming cable ties.
- **Sharp craft knife**, for cutting limbs and trimming vinyl parts.

Screwdriver

This is the best tool I found for prying apart the base doll. You will need to take the head and limbs from your base doll. Most times they are anchored in and are very hard to twist off unless you can get a tool such as a screwdriver under the body to pry them off.

Paint Applicators

- **Artist's paint brushes**, for applying and smoothing paints. You'll use a fan brush for painting inside of the limbs, a round brush for washing paint on the body, and a small flat brush for painting tinted varnish on nails and lips. I also use a script liner for painting eyebrows.
- **Round 3/4" stencil brush** for pouncing color for cheeks and other blushing.
- **Makeup sponges**, for blending paint colors
- **Toothpicks**, for applying glues and dotting paint. (You can also use a **small crochet needle** for attaching eyelashes.)

Sewing Machine

The new cloth body will need to be machine stitched for the best results.

Miscellaneous Tools

- **Funnel**, for filling the weight bags with pellets or sand
- **Plastic measuring cup**, 1/8 cup size with spout, for scooping pellets or sand
- **Rubber gloves**, to protect your hands while you work with chemicals.
- **Metal nail file**, to smooth edges of cable ties.

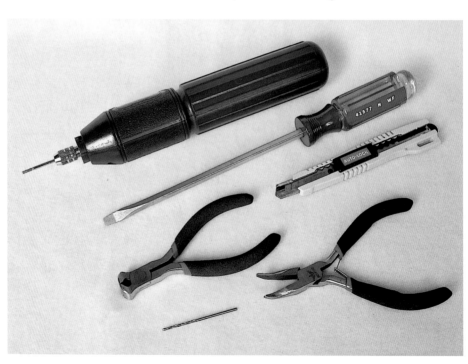

Pictured top to bottom: Dremel® Tool, screwdriver, craft knife, wire cutters, needlenose pliers, drill bit

Coloring Your Doll

Dye

Liquid dyes, the kind used to dye fabric, is needed for dyeing the vinyl parts. You will need wine, pink, tan, or brown, depending upon the skin color you wish to make the doll.

Paints

- **Acrylic craft paints**, lavender or periwinkle, for coloring inside the vinyl doll parts. This gives the limbs depth.
- **Oil paints**, for coloring the outsides of the doll's limbs, torso (if the torso is vinyl), and head. The oil paints penetrate the vinyl, creating a permanent coloration. You can use artist's oil paints, transparent oil paints (which tint the vinyl rather than changing the color), or heat set synthetic oil paints.
- **Pink transparent glass paint**, for coloring lips.
- **Cream stencil paint**, for blushing and shadowing the doll's skin. Choose either a berry color or any red/pink color (your choice) for blushing. Use blue for shadowing. Find cream stencil paint at crafts stores.
- **Burnt sienna oil paint** *or* **fine-tip brown permanent marker**, for painting eyebrows.

- **White or ivory paint marker**, for finishing the nail tips. *Option:* use white or ivory acrylic craft paint and a thin paint brush.

Paint Medium

Refined linseed oil is used for thinning oil paint. Find this in the paint sections of crafts and art supplies stores. It comes in a small bottle, and one bottle will last a long time. You could also use safflower oil, the kind manufactured for use with oil paint, NOT the cooking oil. Neither will yellow with age.

Colored Pencil

Blue watercolor pencil or fine-tip blue marker, for making vein lines

Ink

Stamping ink used with an inkpad can be used to blush cheeks and other areas of dolls.

Varnish

Gloss varnish, for finishing the lips and the nails. *Option:* Use a satin finish varnish for less shine.

Pictured: (1) White and other colors of oil paint; (2) Transparent glass paint; (3) Dye; (4 & 5) Acrylic craft paints; (6) Cream stencil paint; (7) Paint marker; (8) Watercolor pencil for adding veins, (9) Round brush for washing body; (10) Fan brush for painting inside of limbs; (11) Liner brush for detailing.

Eye Supplies

Doll Eyes

You can find doll eyes in a wide range of styles and prices. There is no right or wrong product to use – it's the artist's choice. Have fun experimenting. Use the Eye Chart to select the right size eyes for your doll.

Eye Chart

Doll Size	Eye Size
14"	18 mm round
16"	18-19 mm round
20", 22"	20-21mm round
20", 22"	22mm round
21"	22mm oval

Eyelashes

Doll eyelashes are available where doll making supplies are sold. You may also use false eyelashes from cosmetic departments. For infant dolls, select a sparse, light-colored eyelash. Double lashes (top and bottom) are more realistic, but since some newborn babies do not have bottom lashes, many doll artists apply the top lash only.

Eyebrows can be created with paint or by rooting the curved hairs from a pair of eyelashes. (Read about rooting in the Section on Hair Techniques.)

Glue

Use a white craft ("tacky") glue to attach the eyelash strips.

Gloss Varnish

A super glossy varnish or a glaze is needed to apply to the eye. This will add the extra shine needed for realism. The gloss can also be used to create tears.

Applicators

- **Wooden toothpicks** are a handy aid for applying eyelashes.
- **A thin crochet needle** can also be used to help apply eyelashes and eyes.
- **A small round artist brush** is needed for applying the glaze. You do not need a high quality brush here.

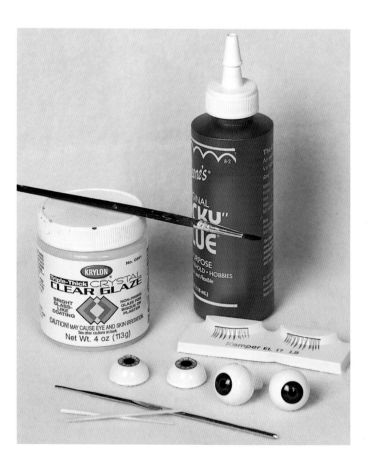

Pictured: Gloss varnish, paint brush for applying varnish, thin crochet needle or toothpicks for adding eyelashes, white glue, eyelashes, two examples of dolls' eyes

Hair Making Supplies

You can add hair to your doll by gluing on a wig or by hand rooting hair.

Doll Wig

These can be found where doll making supplies are sold.

Hair

You will need about 2 oz. quality synthetic or human hair if you wish to root hair to the doll head.

Mohair

Mohair can also be used when you wish to hand root hair. Mohair can be found where doll making supplies are sold. It is labeled "angora mohair" or "goat mohair." It is the actual cut wool – not a yarn.

Tools

- **A rooting tool** for holding the rooting needles

- **4 rooting needles** – 48 gauge barbed felting needles or sewing machine needles. (I prefer the latter; I clip off the pointed ends.)
- **Thinning shears**, for shaping wigs and/or trimming hair after it's applied. (Buy them at drugstores.)

Sock Filled with Rice

Use this for warming the head when rooting the hair. Fill a soft sock with rice until it is the size to almost fill the doll head. Place the sock-filled rice and a small cup of water in the microwave oven until warm. The water adds moisture to the rice. Place rice inside doll head to soften the vinyl – this will make it easier to root the hair.

Decoupage Medium

Use this for sealing the ends of the hair inside the head. *Option:* Silicone sealer.

Pictured: Mohair-straight and curly, wig, rooting tool, needles, thinning shears (for shaping human hair)

Preparing the Doll

To prepare the doll for coloring, it's necessary to first remove the vinyl parts from the doll's body, take off the factory paint from the head and face, and give the doll a bath.

Disassembling the Doll

1. On soft-bodied dolls, cable ties hold the doll's head and limbs on its trunk. You want to get under the tie with a screwdriver and pop off the pieces. Start by using a screwdriver to pry up the doll's head to reveal the tie holding the head. Sometimes you can just "pop" the head or limb from the body by putting pressure on the screwdriver. *Option:* Use snippers or a craft knife to cut the nylon ties from the neck, arms, and legs. **(Photo 1)**

2. Remove the legs and arms the same way – using the screwdriver to pop them off. **(Photo 2)**

3. On vinyl-body dolls, the limbs and head are usually not attached with ties – they are merely fitted into place. On these types of bodies, use a long-shaft screwdriver to get into the joint and pry the limbs off the body. **(Photo 3)** TIP: If your vinyl-body doll feels stiff and you're having a hard time removing the limbs, try soaking the doll in hot water to soften the vinyl. It will come apart more easily.

4. Use a craft knife to enlarge the openings at the ends of the limbs (if needed) so it will be easier to paint inside the limbs and fill them. Simply take your craft knife and cut away a larger circle of the vinyl, leaving an edge around the opening so it can be sealed. **(Photo 4)** *CAUTION: Cut carefully. Craft knives are sharp.*

Removing the Factory Coloring

1. Remove the coloring that represents the hair using a cotton ball dipped in paint remover or acetone. Work from the front hairline to the middle of the head. Don't let the remover run onto the face as it will give a shine to the vinyl. I use the remover sparingly, working from the edges of the "hair" towards the middle of the head in slow movements. Be careful and take your time – this is a lengthy process. Don't be overly concerned with getting the color removed from indentations in the head. Just remove color from the surface. **(Photo 5, Photo 6 – showing color removed)**

2. To remove the face and lip color and all factory blushing on the hands and feet **do not** use acetone – use a multi-purpose paint and adhesive remover. If there is any other factory paint on doll's body or any marks that shouldn't be there, remove them at this time with multi-purpose remover. TIP: Although not shown in this photo, it's a good idea to wear rubber gloves to protect your hands.

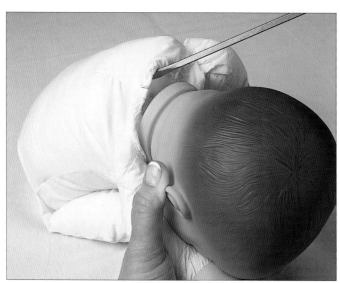

Photo 1 – Removing the head from a soft-bodied doll.

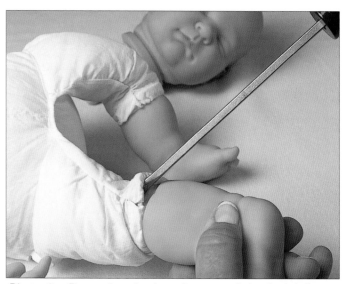

Photo 2 – Removing the legs from a soft-bodied doll.

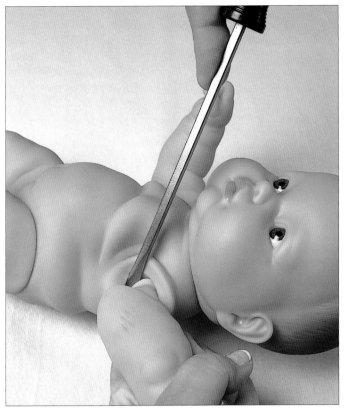

Photo 3 – Removing limbs from a vinyl-body doll.

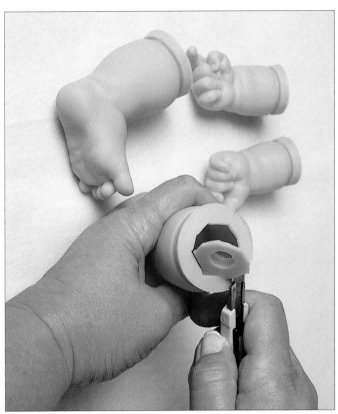

Photo 4 – Enlarging the openings in the limbs of a soft-bodied doll.

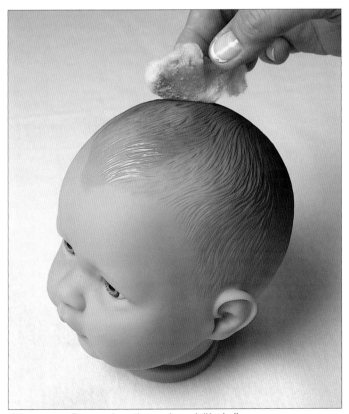

Photo 5 – Removing the painted "hair."

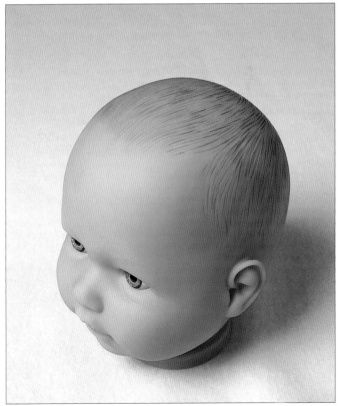

Photo 6 – A doll's head with the hair removed.

Bathing the Doll Parts

Give the vinyl parts of the doll a bath in hot, soapy water. (I use dish detergent.) Let them soak 10 to 15 minutes. This removes the "baby powder" smell some dolls have and removes any waxy finish or residue from the paint remover. Rinse well after soaking. **(Photo 7)**

If your doll is not new, you may need to use a mildly abrasive scrubbing cleanser to clean the body and limbs, and then bathe the doll. There can be a lot of dirt in the vinyl, and you must remove it so the vinyl can absorb the new coloring. Rinse well.

Dyeing the Doll

A dye bath is used to color the vinyl. Use liquid dye only – it comes in a solution so you won't run the risk of having dye powder leave spots or create heavily dyed areas because it did not dissolve completely. The lighter your dye color, the less chance of "bruising" or discoloration. **(See Photo 11)**

When dyeing, aim for a coloration one shade lighter than your desired skin color result because the color will deepen as it dries. TIP: If you're not sure how dark you want your doll to be, dye it in stages. It is much easier to dip again than to try to remove over-dyeing.

1. Fill your sink or a plastic basin with hot tap water. Add the dye to the water and stir to make sure the dye and water are well blended before you put in the body pieces. The limbs need to be fully submerged in the hot dye bath. **(Photo 8)**
   Caucasian doll – Add 1 capful of pink dye and 1 capful of tan dye, and set your timer for 2 minutes. African American or Hispanic doll – Use 2 capfuls of tan and 1 capful of pink and leave the parts in the dye longer – I dye 5 minutes for Hispanic and 9 minutes for African American.
   Option: Test the coloring after you have done several two-minute dips, keeping in mind that the color will darken when the doll has dried. To better judge the color, rinse the doll parts well with cold water.

2. When the correct amount of time has passed or you've determined the color pleases you, remove the doll parts from the dye bath **(Photo 9)** and rinse the pieces with cold water. It's very important to rinse out all the dye. The final rinse water should be clear.

3. Dry the limbs thoroughly. You do not want any moisture left in the limbs as mold or mildew can develop. In the summer months, I set the limbs outside in the sun, and they usually dry in one afternoon. When weather does not permit this, I use the heat from my oven. Here's how: Place a dish towel on a cookie sheet, and put the limbs on the towel. **(Photo 10)** Preheat the oven to 350 degrees, then turn off the oven. Put the cookie sheet with the doll parts in the oven and leave in the oven overnight. CAUTION: The oven method is safe and easy, but be sure the oven is turned off before you put in the doll parts. **Do not use a microwave oven.** A microwave oven will ruin the doll parts.
   Other options: There are drying racks available that hold the limbs vertically for drying. Or design a rack of your own.

Photo 7 – Bathing the doll parts.

Photo 8 – Dyeing vinyl parts in a dye bath.

Photo 9 – Removing the parts from the dye bath.

Photo 10 – Drying doll parts on a cookie sheet.

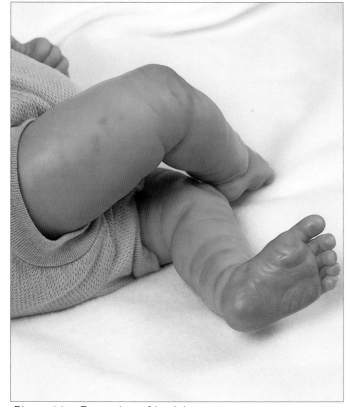

Photo 11 – Examples of bruising.

Bruising

Bruising happens if the dye is not mixed properly or is left in the limbs too long – the color works through the vinyl and appears as a black and blue mark on the doll, sometimes a year or more later. To prevent bruising, use liquid dye only, dilute the dye completely with water, and rinse thoroughly. **(Photo 11)**

Adding New Eyes

The next step is to remove the doll's eyes and put in new ones. Warming the head to soften it makes it easy to remove the old eyes and install new ones.

1. Place the doll's head in a glass bowl of boiling water for about a minute. Remove the head from the bowl of water and, using a cloth towel to hold the head, shake the excess water from the head. While the head is warm, pop out the eyes with your hand. **(Photo 12)**
   Option: Insert the end of a wooden spoon in the head and submerge the head in a pan of boiling water for 90 seconds, taking great care to not let the vinyl touch the pan, then shake out the water. Use a dry dish towel to protect your fingers as you insert them in the head and push out the original eyes. They should come out easily.

2. Dry the eye sockets – you do not want any water in the back of the eye as this can cause mold to grow. I use a hair dryer to dry the eye sockets – the heat keeps them pliable, too. You can also use a dish towel.

3. Use your fingers to push in the new eyes – just insert them at an angle and push them into the doll's warm head. Position the eyes to your satisfaction. **(Photo 13)** Make sure the white area around each iris is even **(Photo 14)** so you won't have a cross-eyed doll. TIP: Stand back and look at the eyes, then adjust as needed.

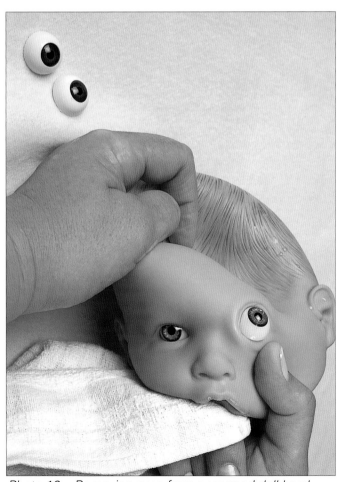

Photo 12 – Removing eyes from a warmed doll head.

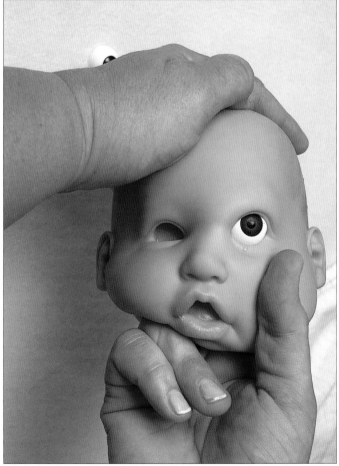

Photo 13 – Inserting new eyes.

4. Fill the head with cold water and place it in the sink. This will harden the vinyl and keep the eyes in place. Allow the inside of the head to drain and dry naturally on a paper towel.

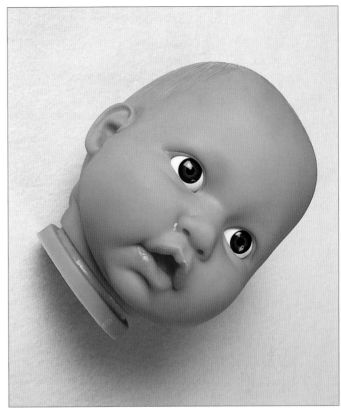

Photo 14 – A head with new eyes in place.

Recycling Dolls' Eyes

Most doll makeover artists throw away the eyes they remove from their play dolls, but the eyes can be repainted and used again if you have the patience and time to work on them. It takes practice, but once you have done a couple of pairs, you will have mastered this art. This is a nice way to recycle the eyes and have a one-of-a-kind doll. It's my experience that dolls with custom-painted eyes sell for a higher price.

I like to paint the eyes I'm recycling with colors that are not found in commercially available doll's eyes, such as teal, turquoise, or metallic blue. (Metallic colors give such depth to eyes – they sparkle and seem so real!)

Here's How to Repaint Dolls' Eyes:

1. Soak the eyes in water so you can remove the paper backing that covers the iris and pupil portion of the eye.

2. Dip a cotton swab in multi-purpose remover or acetone. Remove the color from the iris and pupil, rubbing with the swab in a circular motion and being careful to not touch the whites of the eye as you work. Continue working in a circular motion until all color is removed.

3. Rinse the eye and let dry completely.

4. Dip the end of a round toothpick in black acrylic paint and put a dot of black paint in the center of each eye. This will be the pupil. Try to match the size and location of the pupils for a perfect pair of eyes. Let dry completely.

5. Paint the iris with a color of your choice. Let dry completely.

6. Apply clear varnish to protect the eye color. Let dry.

7. Insert the eyes. ❑

Recoloring the Doll

I use color inside the limbs and on the outside of the limbs and head. The color on the inside shows through faintly, tinting and defining the creases in the toes and fingers.

Painting Inside the Doll

Adding color inside the doll isn't mandatory, but it does add to the realistic look of the finished doll. I use very thin coats of acrylic craft paint to color the insides of the doll parts. These are the colors I recommend:
- Light-skinned doll – Periwinkle blue
- Medium- or dark-skinned doll – Lavender

TIP: When you shop for paints you may see various tones of these colors. A light tint is the best choice.

1. *Inside the head:* If you are using a wig for your doll, paint the inside of your doll's head, using a fan brush. **(Photo 15)** If you are rooting hair, you'll want to paint inside the head after the rooting is done. (Read about rooting in the Section on Hair Techniques.)

2. *Inside the limbs:* Again using a fan brush, carefully paint inside the limbs. Put two thin coats of paint inside of the limbs, one now and one in 24 hours. It's a challenge to get the color into all the small places, but you should be able to reach them with the fan brush. **(Photo 16)**

Color Washing the Outside

Color washing creates the doll's lifelike skin tone. In this step, oil paints are applied to the outsides of the doll's limbs, body (if the body is vinyl), and head. The paints penetrate the vinyl, creating a permanent coloration that cannot be achieved by blushing alone. You can use artist's oil paints, transparent oil paints (which tint the vinyl rather than changing the color), or heat set synthetic oil paints.

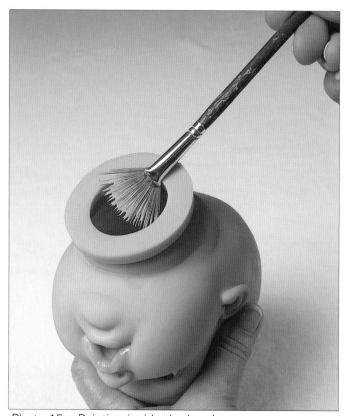

Photo 15 – Painting inside the head.

Photo 16 – Painting inside the limbs with a fan brush.

I use one of two color mixes, depending on the skin tone I want on the doll. Both are mixed and applied the same way. On dolls that have darker skin coloring, I mix a pale pink color; on lighter-skinned dolls, I use a light blue wash. (If you look closely at a baby's skin, you'll discover it does have a blue undertone, and some doll artists use only light blue.)

Try the colors and see what you like best. I like the idea that no doll is exactly the same, and I like to experiment with the coloring.

1. Mix the oil paint, using a cotton swab. Thin the paint to a wash consistency with the thinner the paint manufacturer recommends. I use three parts paint and one part refined linseed oil. DO NOT use cooking oil or baby oil as a thinner – they will become gummy over time. **(Photo 17)**

2. Working one piece of the doll at a time, use a soft natural bristle round brush to apply the color mixture to the outside of the limbs and face. **(Photo 18)** Use the brush to pounce color into the crevices. **(Photo 19)**

3. After applying the paint, use a paper towel to remove the excess paint. **(Photo 20)**

4. Then use an old sock, a makeup sponge or a piece of a t-shirt to smooth and remove more paint. Leave enough paint for a soft look. **(Photo 21)**

5. Use a cotton swab to remove the heavy application of color from the creases and deep crevices. Aim for a natural look (not white and chalky). **(Photo 22)** Use a paint brush to smooth the paint in detailed areas. **(Photo 23)**

6. When you've finished one body part, move on to the next. **(Photo 24)** Allow at least one week for the oil paints to cure and dry completely.

Blushing

The blushing process involves applying paint and color to the creases and folds in the doll's body to achieve a natural look. With blushing, the feet and hands come to life, and the process is fun! Three blushing methods are discussed in this section. Try them all and decide which you like best.

Where to Apply Blushing? Raised areas of the doll's body need the most blushing. TIP: Collect pictures of newborn babies that you can study and refer to when you blush the doll.

Continued on page 27

Photo 17 – Using a cotton swab to mix oil paint for color washing.

Photo 18 – Using a brush to apply the color wash to all vinyl doll parts.

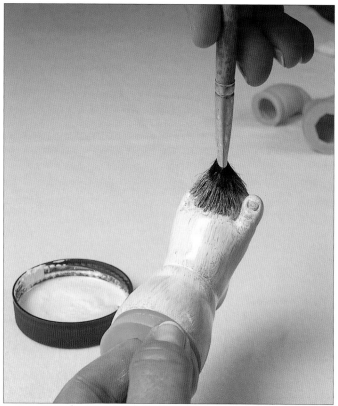

Photo 19 – Pouncing color into the crevices around the toes using a soft round brush

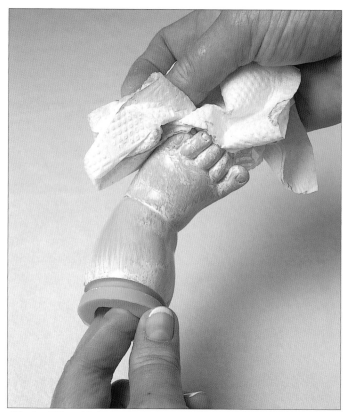

Photo 20 – Using a paper towel to remove most of the paint. But don't remove all the paint – the goal is a soft look

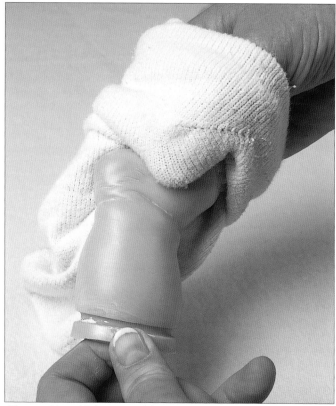

Photo 21 – Using an old sock to smooth the paint and remove the excess.

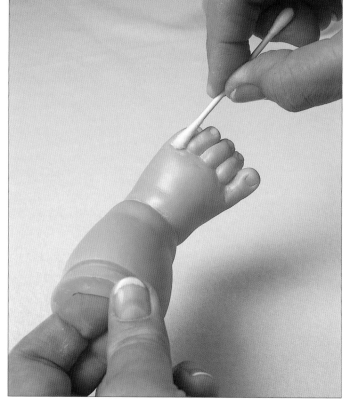

Photo 22 – Using a cotton swab to smooth paint in the creases of the toes.

Blushing,
Continued from page 25

• **Hands** – Blush the palms of the hands, the knuckles of the fingers, and the backs of the hands. The tips of the fingers also look nice when color is applied to them.

• **Feet** – Blush both tops and bottoms. I use more color on the outside edges of the feet and less in the center of the bottom of the foot. The back of the heel requires blushing, and so do the bends in the toes. Add blush around the ankles and in the fat creases above the back of the foot.

• **Body** – Blush all the areas that attract attention, such as the fat tummy area, the bottom, the knees, and the fat folds below the arms. I use paint on the belly button to make it darker.

• **Face** – The cheeks are the most important part of the face. I also add blush to the tip of the nose, the ears, and the top of the natural rise of the eyebrow.

Stencil Paint Blushing

Cream stencil paint comes in a jar and, as its name implies, it is a creamy (as opposed to liquid or gel) paint used for stenciling. I like to apply cream stencil paint with my fingers and with brushes. I use a berry color paint. NOTE: Don't use liquid acrylic paint – you can't get the same effect.

1. Rub your index finger over the stencil paint and apply it to the doll, placing more color in the creases and on the fat rolls of the doll. **(Photo 25)**

2. Use your thumb to blend the color. **(Photo 26)**

Continued on page 29

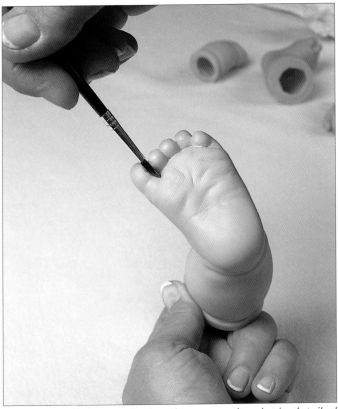

Photo 23 – Using a paint brush to smooth paint in detailed areas.

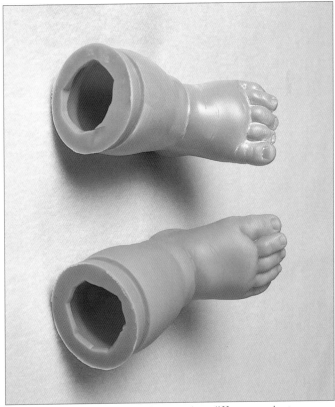

Photo 24 – This photo shows the difference between a foot that has been washed with color (top) and one that has not (bottom).

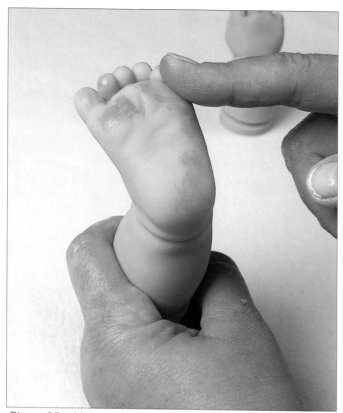

Photo 25 – Using a finger to rub cream stencil paint on the pads of the feet.

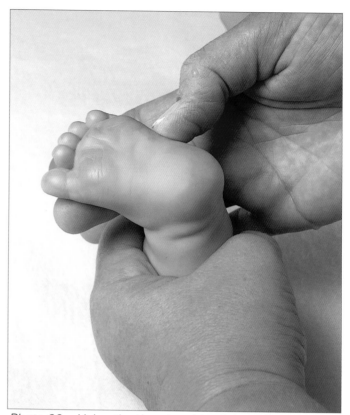

Photo 26 – Using the thumb to blend the paint.

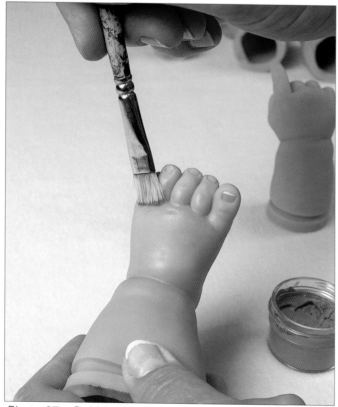

Photo 27 – Dabbing on paint with stiff-bristled flat brush.

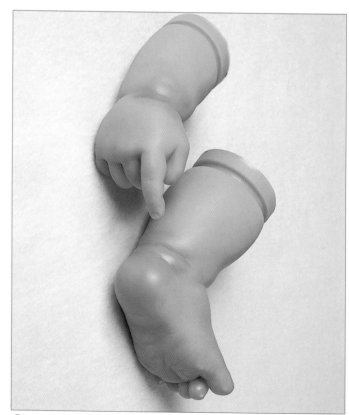

Photo 28 – Finished legs and arms.

Continued from page 27

Brush Application – Two Techniques

I use a round 3/4" stencil brush (or other stiff-bristle brush) and a small flat bristle brush to apply layers of color. Practice (and practice) until you achieve the look you want.

Pouncing:

The lifelike texture of a blotchy skin tone is achieved by pouncing with a stiff-bristle brush.

1. Pour some rubbing alcohol in a dish or small jar. Dip the stencil brush in rubbing alcohol and blot on a paper bag or paper towel.

2. Dip the brush in the stencil paint color and lightly pounce the color on the doll's limbs until the color and texture of the blushing pleases you. Repeat this process to create layers of blushing and to apply blushing to all the limbs. Blend any excess color with a makeup sponge or your fingers.

Stroking:

Use a small paint brush to stroke color in the deep creases, making sure the color blends with the other blushing you have done. **(Photo 27)** When the blushing is complete, let the paints cure at least 24 hours.

Dry Blushing

Dry blushing is like the painting technique known as dry brushing, where a bristle brush is loaded with paint and most of the paint is removed from the brush before it is applied to the surface. For dry blushing, you need acrylic or oil paint and a dry brush paint brush, available at crafts stores. This brush has stiff bristles for scrubbing but still bends freely.

1. Load the brush with paint, then dab the brush on a brown paper bag until most of the paint is removed and the brush is almost dry.

2. Lightly brush the paint left in the brush to the blushing areas.

Ink Blushing

A third method of blushing uses an inkpad with stamping ink. You will need a new, clean makeup sponge and a pink or rose-color pigment inkpad from a crafts store.

1. Use your finger to place a dab of the blush color on the area you want to blush. **(Photo 29)**

2. Use the makeup sponge to spread and smooth out the color. Add more color as needed to achieve the desired blush effect.

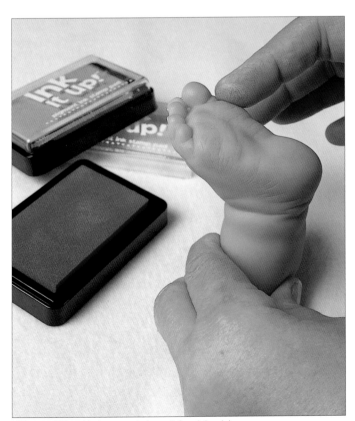

Photo 29 – Using an inkpad for blushing.

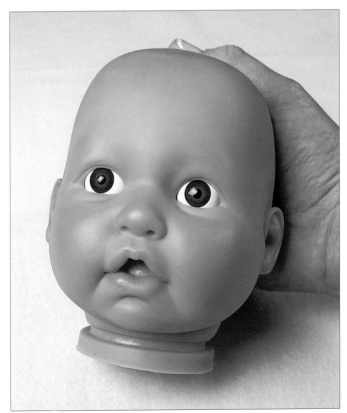

Photo 30 – A finished blushed head.

Adding Details & Features

Veining & Shadowing

I use a blue watercolor pencil or a fine-tip blue marker to add lines that look like veins on the temples at the sides of the head **(Photo 31)**, on the wrists, and on the bottoms of the feet. You can add veining on the inside or outside of the doll, but I find I have better control working on the outside. The lines should be faint and barely visible so they look realistic.

I use blue stencil paint for shadowing on the tops of the eyelids, on the bridge of the nose, and at the bottom center of feet. *Option:* On the narrow bridge of the nose, make a line with a blue marker and soften with rubbing alcohol.

Painting Eyebrows

The eyebrows frame the eyes. To paint the eyebrows, choose a brow color that complements the hair color and is a slightly darker tone than the hair. Burnt sienna oil paint thinned with linseed oil is a good choice. Use a 4/0 or 5/0 script liner artist brush to paint the very fine lines of the eyebrows. I use wax paper or a glass plate as a painting palette. (The slicker the surface, the easier it is to load a small amount of paint on your brush.) TIP: Place the doll's head upside down in your lap or on a table – this position makes it easier to work.

1. Locate the raised areas above the eyes on your doll where the eyebrows will be painted. To guide your strokes, draw a light pencil line from the corner of the nose to the inside corner of the eye or mark guidelines with pieces of tape. **(Photo 32)**

2. Load the brush with a small amount of paint. Do a couple practice brush strokes on the palette – you want to make very thin, short strokes.

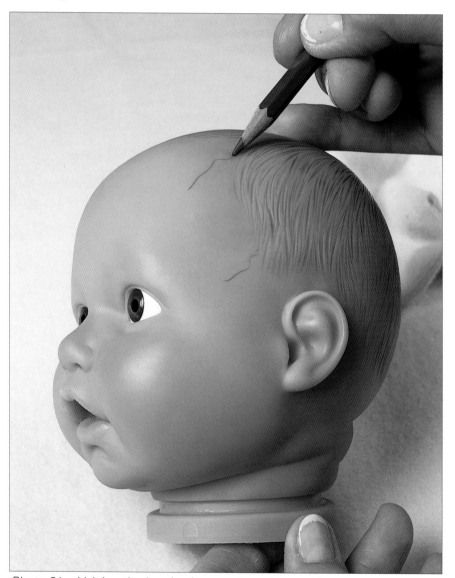

Photo 31 – Veining the head using a watercolor pencil.

3. Start your strokes at the brow line, which is straight up from the outer edge of the doll's nostrils. Barely touching the tip of the brush to the doll's head, paint the eyebrows. **(Photo 33)** Each stroke is a single hair and should be wispy and light.

Option: You can also add eyebrows by micro rooting. (For more information about rooting, see the sections that follow on "Rooting Hair" and "Attaching Eyelashes.")

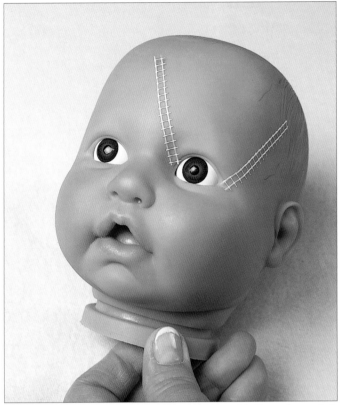

Photo 32 – Pieces of tape placed as guidelines for painting eyebrows.

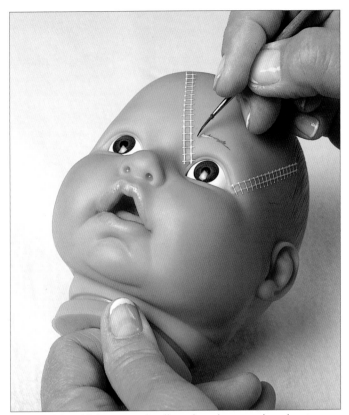

Photo 33 – Using a script liner brush to make short, very light strokes for eyebrows.

Painting Nails

There are two steps to complete the nails – adding white lines at the nail tips and applying tinted varnish to the nails.

To make the lines at the nail tips, use a thin liner brush and white or ivory acrylic paint. (I prefer ivory – white tends to look too bright.) Paint a thin line on the very tip of each fingernail and toenail. **(Photo 34)** This gives a "French manicure" look. *Option:* Use a fine-tip ivory or white paint marker. **(Photo 35)**

To paint the nails, I use matte sheen acrylic varnish (you can use satin sheen varnish, if you prefer) tinted with a small amount of plum or ruby red transparent glass paint. You want only a tint of color – the mixture should be almost clear. I mix 8 drops of varnish with 1 drop of paint. Use a brush to apply one coat at a time on the nail beds. **(Photo 36)** When you are pleased with the amount of color, seal the nails with clear varnish. **(Photo 37)** I use as many as three coats of tinted color. You can add as many coats of clear varnish as you like. The more coats you add, the lighter the color will appear.

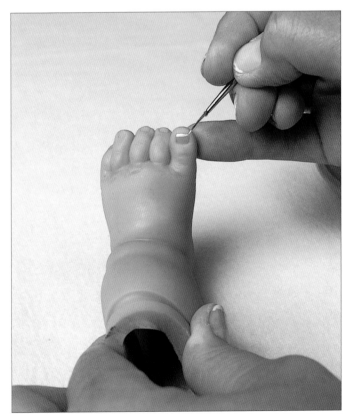

Photo 34 – Adding lines of soft white paint at the tips of the toenails with a brush.

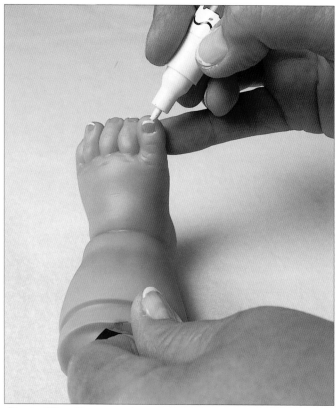

Photo 35 – You can also use a paint marker to make the lines.

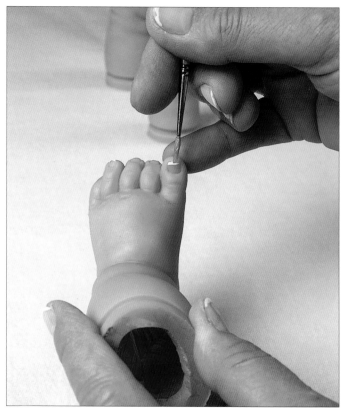

Photo 36 – Adding a tinted overglaze to toenails.

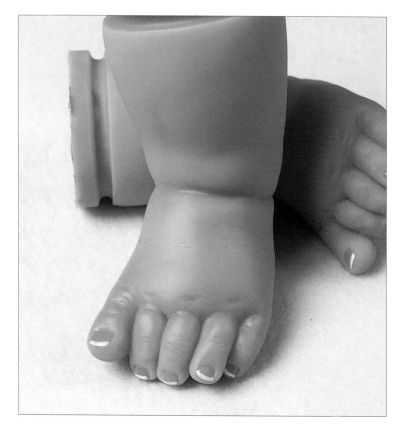

Photo 37 – Toenails are complete.

Painting Lips

The technique for painting the lips is similar to painting the nails – you mix a very light tint of color and apply it one coat at a time. You can use the same transparent glass paint color paint you used for the nails – just use a little more paint with the varnish. The resulting color should look natural and sheer.

1. Use a liner brush to apply the tinted varnish, one coat at a time. **(Photo 38)** Let the lips dry completely before you apply another layer.

2. When the final layer of lip color has dried, apply a sealer of clear gloss varnish (for a wet look) or clear satin varnish (for a softer look).

3. *Option:* A thin line of a darker tint, similar to a lip liner, can be applied around the outer lip area. This makes the lips stand out a little better and creates depth.

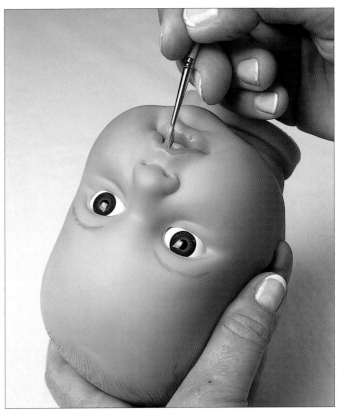

Photo 38 – Painting the lips.

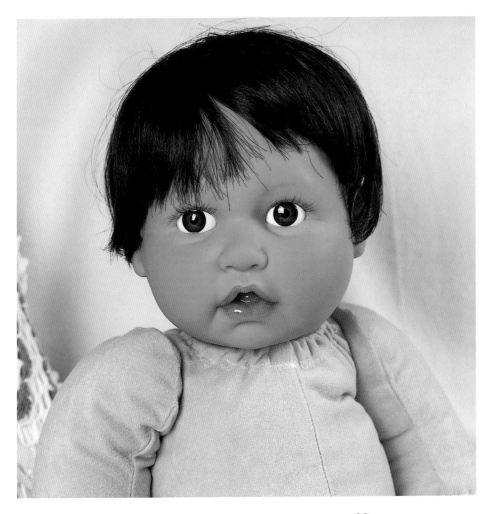

Hair Techniques

This section shows you two techniques for adding hair to your doll – attaching a wig and hand rooting.

Attaching a Wig

There are many wig options available, including mohair, human hair, and synthetic fibers such as viscose. **Mohair wigs** are made of goat hair. They have a nice natural curl and come in a variety of colors. You can also wet the wig with water, apply hair gel, and scrunch the hair for a curlier appearance. I like using mohair wigs with clear caps – they look so natural. **Human hair wigs** are made of real hair, which is thicker than mohair. They can be straight or curly and come in a variety of colors. **Synthetic hair wigs** are available in a variety of colors and textures. My preferred synthetic is viscose, which feels silky and looks shiny. A rule of thumb is to choose a wig color that coordinates with the doll's eye color and skin color.

Wigs come in various sizes – you will need to measure the circumference of the doll's head to see what size your doll needs. **(Photo 39)** To attach a wig, use a good multi-purpose glue that dries clear or a thick white tacky glue.

1. Place the wig on the doll's head, adjusting it until you like the way it is positioned. **(Photo 40)**
   TIP: I hold the wig in place with a large quilting pin that I place through the center of the wig into the doll's head.

2. When you're pleased with how the wig looks, take a pencil or fine-tip marker and mark the doll's head at the edge of the wig's cap. **(Photo 41)** This is your guide for applying the glue. Remove the wig.

Continued on page 36

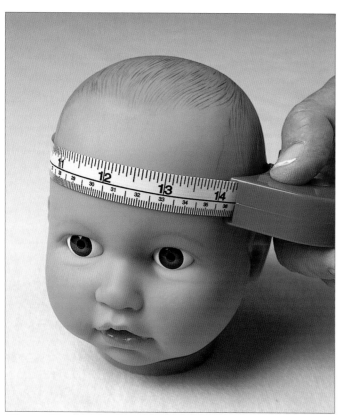

Photo 39 – Measuring the doll's head.

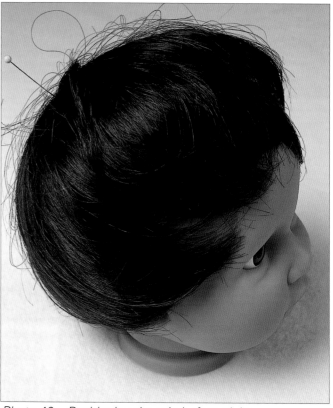

Photo 40 – Positioning the wig before gluing.

Photo 41 – Marking the placement of the wig cap.

Photo 42 – Applying glue to the head.

Photo 43 – Using a brush to smooth and spread the glue.

Photo 44 – Positioning the wig over the glue.

Continued from page 34

3. Apply glue inside the marked lines over the entire area of the doll's head that the wig will cover. **(Photo 42)** Use a brush to smooth and spread the lines of glue. **(Photo 43)**

4. Starting at the back, slowly apply the wig to the head, aligning it with the marked lines. **(Photo 44)** Press firmly to make sure the wig is adhered firmly to the scalp. TIP: If you get glue on the hair, use a wet washcloth to remove the glue before it dries.

5. Let the wig dry in place overnight – it may take 24 hours or more for the glue to set up completely. When the glue is dry, you can trim the hair or thin it with thinning shears.

Rooting Hair

Rooting is fun, but it takes time. (It's called micro rooting when you apply only one to two strands of hair each time you insert the rooting needle.) The finer and fewer the strands, the more realistic the hair will look. You must have great patience to hand root as the process involves placing hundreds of strands all over the head, but the results are well worth the effort. For a natural look when rooting, mix several hair colors – the color variation looks more realistic.

If you are rooting light-colored hair or micro rooting, you need to remove the hair lines from the head, using a multi-purpose hand tool with the sanding attachment. It takes time to remove all the lines, but it's necessary. TIP: Work outside – this is a really messy job, and the vinyl shavings can get everywhere.

Fiber Choices:

For best results, I recommend premium mohair, viscose, or human hair for rooting.

Premium mohair is my favorite. It works well with both felting and rooting needles and gives a natural look. Mohair comes straight, wavy, or curly. I like wavy mohair; when a no-tangle spray is applied you have the most beautiful wave. Try to find clean,

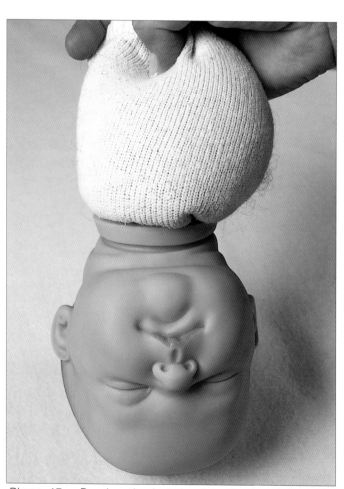

Photo 45 – Pouring the hot rice into the head from the sock.

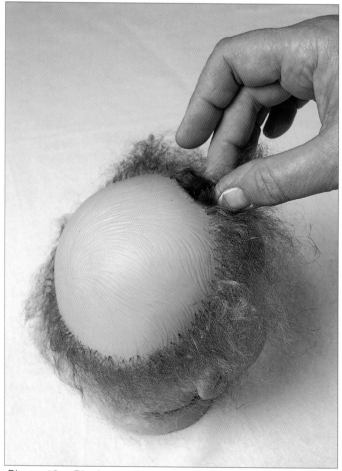

Photo 46 – Placing a piece of mohair on the head.

combed mohair that's ready to use. You can also dye mohair with tea. Don't buy processed mohair – it is usually too dry and brittle. Buy the actual cut wool, not a yarn.

A synthetic fiber, **viscose** is often called "man-made silk" because it feels silky soft and looks shiny. It comes two ways – in a continuous filament fiber (the one you want to buy) or a staple fiber (the one you **don't** want to buy). Staple fiber is made from small short fibers that are twisted together; it's hard to root with and the short fibers will make you sneeze.

Quality **human hair** gives a very natural look. It is much thicker than mohair and tends to stand up when you are rooting it, but it can be trained. I have found when I use conditioner on human hair after rooting it lays nicely.

Rooting Procedure:

There are many rooting tools available. I use a resin-handled rooting tool and a lightweight sewing machine needle. The handle has an opening that adjusts to fit the size of the needle. I use needlenose pliers to snip off the pointed tip of the needle through the eye. This leaves a forked end on the needle that works great for rooting.

1. The head is easier to root if the vinyl is warm. To warm the head, I fill an old sock with rice and heat the rice-filled sock with a small glass of water in the microwave for three minutes. (The water adds moisture to the rice as it heats.) CAUTION: The rice-filled sock will be very hot – use an oven mitt to remove it from the oven. Place the open end of the hot rice-filled sock inside the head. The rice will fall into the head. **(Photo 45)** Plug the neck opening with a dry washcloth to keep the heat (and the rice) in. *Option:* Heat the head with a hair dryer to soften the vinyl and make the needle easier to insert.

Continued on page 38

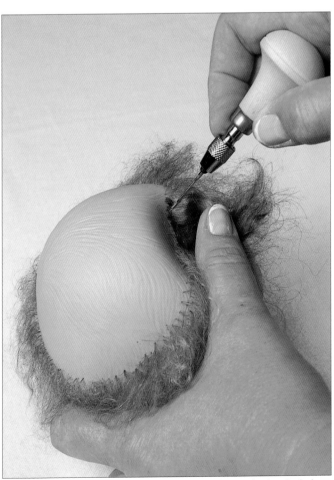

Photo 47 – Pushing the rooting tool through the hair into the head.

Photo 48 – Front view of the doll's head with rooted hair around the edges.

Continued from page 37

2. To start rooting, work from the outside of the head beginning at the forehead. Cut a piece of mohair 1-1/2" long and 1" wide. Position the hair on the head and fan out the hair with your fingers. **(Photo 46)**

3. Hold the hair piece in place with one hand. With the other hand, press the rooting tool into the head. **(Photo 47)** Keep your rooting needle at an angle so the hair will lay down. Work around the head in a circle. **(Photo 48, Photo 49)** Continue until you reach the center of the doll's head. *Option:* If you want the hair to have swirls, change the angle of the tool and the direction by poking the needle in small circles.

4. To finish your rooting job, seal the *inside* of the head with any durable waterproof finish that dries clear, such as silicone sealer or decoupage medium. This will adhere the hair and seal all the openings created by the rooting needle. Don't use a tinted sealer – the color can bleed through.

5. When the sealer is dry, you can trim the hair with scissors.

Option: Use hair gel or mousse for a wet look. You can style the hair with your fingers and create curls. **(Photo 50)**

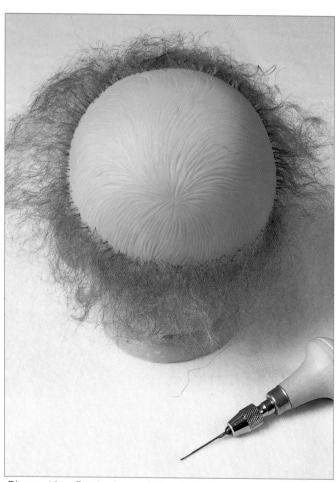

Photo 49 – Back view of the doll's head with rooted hair around the edges.

Photo 50 – The curly wet look, achieved with hair gel or mousse.

Attaching Eyelashes

You can apply eyelashes in a strip or root the individual hairs from a set of eyelashes. (This is called "micro rooting because you are only applying one or two hairs each time you insert the needle.)

Attaching Eyelash Strips

1. Trim the eyelash strips so they are sparse and realistic-looking.

2. Working one strip at a time, apply a fine line of white craft ("tacky") glue along the edge of the eyelash or on the area where you are going to place the eyelash. Use a tool with a fine point, such as a crochet needle or the end of a seam ripper, to push the eyelash into place. **(Photo 51)** Let dry.

3. Use a brush to apply a coat of gloss varnish on the entire eye, working it into the eyelash. **(Photo 52)** This secures the eyelash, attaching it permanently. I also like the wet look that varnish gives the eye.

Rooting Eyelashes and Eyebrows

Eyelashes also can be micro rooted into the crease of the eye. Use individual hairs from a set of eyelashes, and don't trim them before applying. The ones on "sleeping" dolls (dolls with closed eyes) are easiest to do.

Eyebrows can be micro rooted. (I warn you, this is difficult and tedious.) Insert the hairs, one at a time, at an angle, then trim with small curved scissors (the type used for trimming a baby's nails).

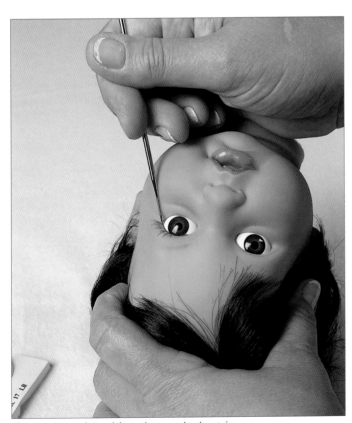

Photo 51 – Attaching the eyelash strip.

Photo 52 – Brushing varnish on the eye.

Creating the Nose

For a more realistic-looking doll, you can make nostril openings. This is called "sculpting the nose" or making the doll a "breather." Gluing a piece of black felt behind the openings ensures the stuffing will not show.

1. Drill a pilot hole for each nostril, using a small drill bit. **(Photo 53)** Be careful – you don't want to damage the doll's face.

2. Use a slightly larger bit to enlarge the holes. **(Photo 54)** The heat of the drilling melts the vinyl as the bit rotates so the hole is nice and round. TIP: Don't turn on the tool until you've placed it in the pilot hole.

3. Clean out the holes with a toothpick. Make sure that no vinyl shreds are still attached and that the openings are clear.

4. Cut a piece of black felt large enough to cover the holes from behind. To check the size, place the felt piece across the drilled holes. **(Photo 55)**

5. Put a small dot of white craft glue on the back of the felt piece and drop the felt piece into the head as close to the nose as possible. **(Photo 56)** Use the eraser end of a pencil or the handle end of a paint brush to guide and press the felt piece into place. Hold the head up to the light to make sure the nostrils are covered; then tap the felt with the eraser end of the pencil. Let dry thoroughly.

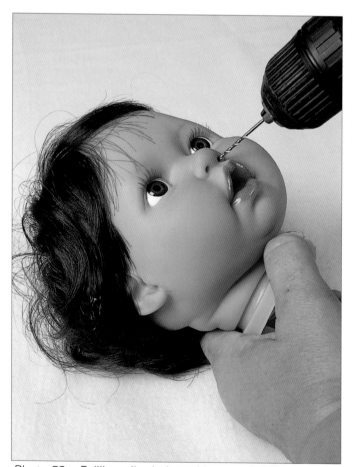

Photo 53 – Drilling pilot holes with a small drill bit.

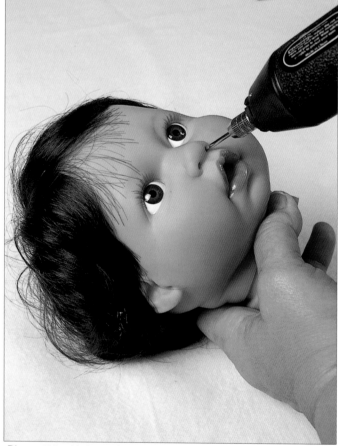

Photo 54 – Using a larger drill bit in the pilot holes to make the openings.

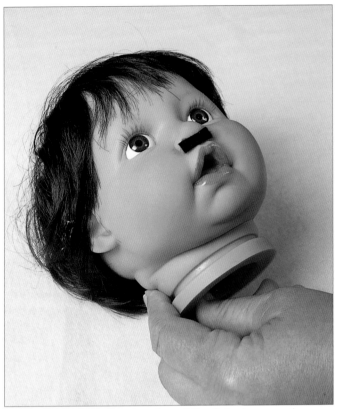

Photo 55 – Checking the size of the felt piece on the nostrils.

Photo 56 – Dropping the felt piece inside the head.

Photo 57 – Using a pencil to position the felt piece behind the nostrils.

Making Bodies

The made-over dolls in this book have soft cloth torsos that are made by the body patterns provided at the back of this book. Their limbs are either full vinyl limbs or partial vinyl limbs attached to partial cloth limbs. These soft cloth bodies have the shape and feel of a real baby. Weight bags aree added to the cloth bodies to make the doll heavier and more realistic. When the doll is dressed, the cloth body doesn't show. This section shows you how to make new bodies and to put the bodies together.

Doll bodies can be **jointed** and **unjointed**. A jointed body allows you to pose (and keep) the doll in realistic positions. Unjointed dolls can also be posed, but they can't stay in some positions like a jointed doll can.

You can make a new soft flannel or doeskin body for your doll or if your purchased doll has a cloth body, you can re-assemble the doll using the original body. One consideration is the quality of the original body. The body that comes on a less expensive doll is usually of poor quality and made of a lightweight fabric, and it may not be jointed. Higher priced dolls have nicer quality bodies and usually are jointed.

Body Patterns

Patterns for doll bodies of various sizes appear at the end of the book. There are two basic types of patterns – one type to accommodate partial vinyl limbs; and one type for trunk-style bodies where you will have full vinyl limbs. The patterns for trunk-style bodies are labeled according to the size of the doll; choose the body size that is in proportion to your doll's head and limbs.

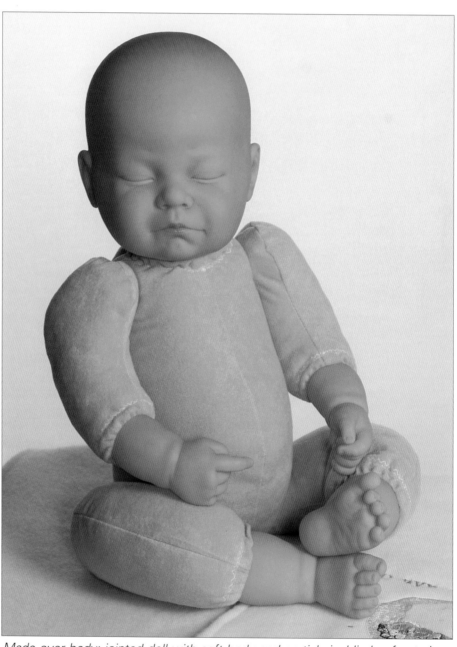

Made over body: jointed doll with soft body and partial vinyl limbs, front view; newborn size

The patterns for jointed dolls with partial vinyl limbs are in two sizes, preemie and newborn, and are appropriate for dolls of various sizes. Preemies are 18-19" long; newborns are 22-24" long. The total length depends on the size of the doll's head – some heads are larger than others. Decide what size body you want to use, keeping in mind the proportion of the finished doll.

As a general guideline, the newborn body will fit newborn-size clothing; the preemie body will fit preemie-size clothing.

Made over body: full-limb doll with soft trunk style body, front view; newborn size

Suggested Body Sizes

Here are some suggested body sizes for dolls with partial vinyl limbs:
16" doll – Use the preemie size body for a finished length of 18"-19"
17" doll – Use the preemie size body for a finished length of 18"-19"
20" doll – Use the newborn size body for a finished length of 21"-22"

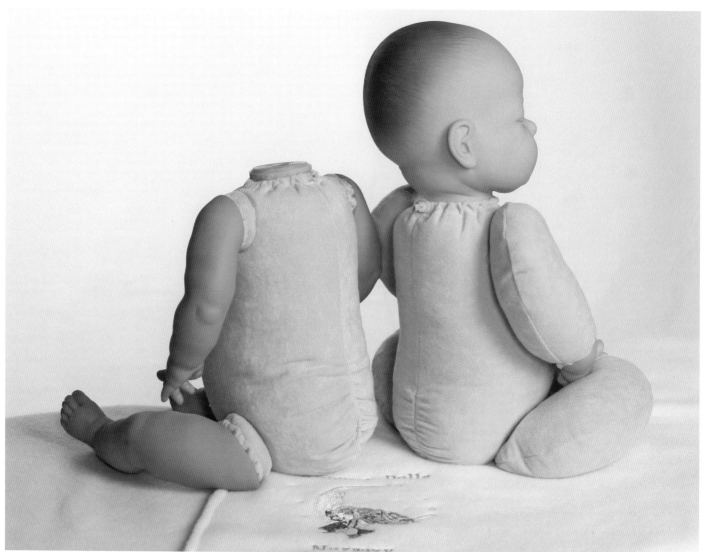

Made over bodies, back views: pictured left to right, full-limb doll with trunk-style body; jointed doll with soft body and partial vinyl limbs. Both dolls are newborn size.

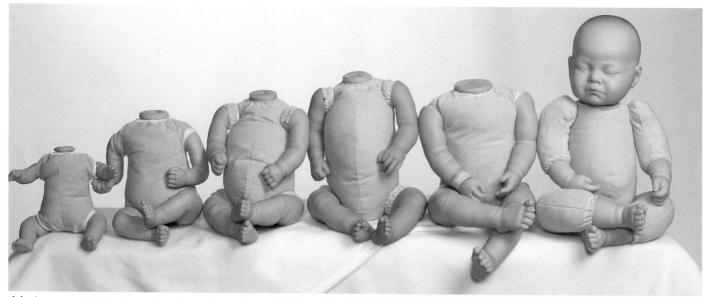

Made over doll bodies of various sizes, from 8" (far left) to newborn size (far right), viewed from the front. All the dolls have full vinyl limbs except the one at the far right.

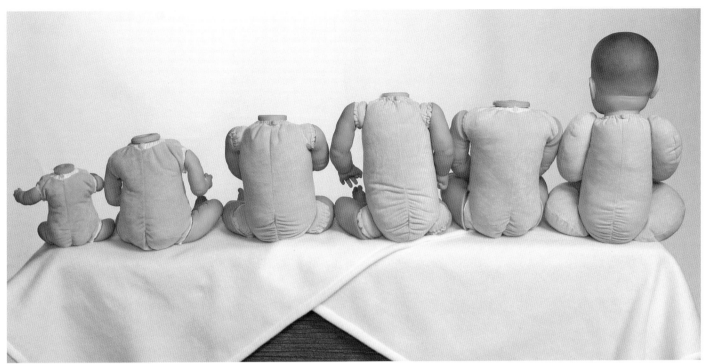

Made over doll bodies of various sizes, from 8" (far left) to newborn size (far right), viewed from the back. All the dolls have full vinyl limbs except the one at the far right.

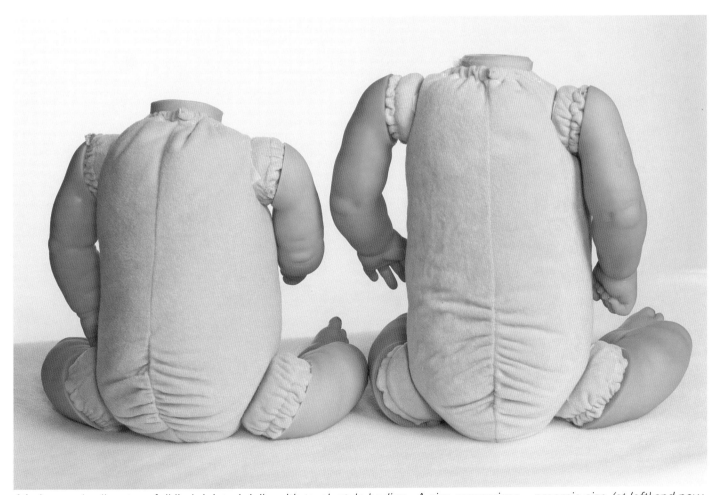

Made over bodies: two full-limb jointed dolls with trunk style bodies. A size comparison – preemie size (at left) and newborn size (at right). Additional fabric pieces have been improvised to cover plastic joints.

Jointed Body with Partial Vinyl Limbs

This section shows you, step by step, how to make a jointed cloth body for a doll with partial vinyl limbs. The fabric body and limbs are sewn using a sewing machine.

Supplies Needed

See the Supplies section for photos and detailed information about supplies.

- Vinyl doll's head and partial vinyl limbs, ready to re-assemble
- 1/2 yard of white or other color (pink, tan, brown) flannel, for the soft body parts
- Light-colored, tightly woven fabric for the weight bag (You can use scraps of the body fabric, if you like.)
- White felt, for sealing the limbs
- Matching thread, cotton/polyester blend (same color as body fabric)
- 1 pair 45mm joints (for the legs)
- 1 pair 35mm joints (for the arms)
- Thin nylon cable ties – four 8" long, one 14" long
- 4" of elastic, 1/8" wide
- Heavy duty non-woven fusible interfacing

- Disappearing fabric marker
- Plastic pellets *or* sterilized sand to add weight to body
- Polyester stuffing
- Plastic measuring cup, 1/8 cup size with spout
- Funnel
- Needlenose pliers
- Wire cutters
- White craft glue
- Metal nail file *or* emery board, for smoothing the cut ends of cable ties
- Tracing paper and pencil
- Transfer paper and tracing wheel
- Scissors

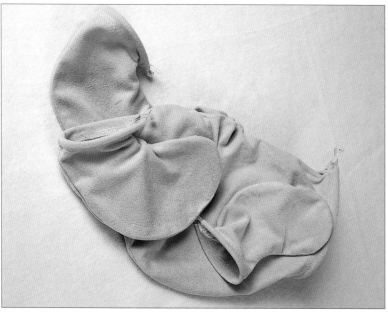

Photo 58 – The sewn pieces of a jointed cloth body

Photo 59 – Slide the cable ties in the casings on the arms, legs, and neck.

Cut & Sew the Body

1. Locate the pattern pieces for the size doll you are making. Trace the patterns from book, then transfer to flannel fabric.

2. Cut out the legs, arms, and torso sections. Cut out the pieces of fusible interfacing that will be used to reinforce the joint areas on the arms, legs, and torso – two for the legs, two for the arms, and two for the torso.

3. Using a disappearing fabric marker, designate which arm and leg pieces will be the inner sides of the arms and legs.

4. Fuse the iron-on interfacing to the joint areas of the torso and the inner sides of the arms and legs. Let cool. Mark the openings with an "x" and clip the openings for the joints.

5. With right sides together, sew the arm pieces together, beginning at inside arm and continuing to single notch. Press the seam.

6. Fold down the arm openings 3/8" and stitch. Finish the raw edge with a zig-zag stitch. (This creates the casing for the cable ties that attach the arm to the body.) Stitch the rest of the arm seam up to the casings, leaving the openings on each end of the casing. Backstitch to secure. Finish the seams with a zig-zag stitch. Turn and press.

7. With right sides together, sew the leg pieces together, beginning the seam as indicated on pattern, and sewing up to notch. Press the seam.

8. Fold down the leg openings 3/8" and stitch. Finish the raw edge with a zig-zag stitch. (This creates the casing for the cable tie that attaches the leg to the body.) Stitch the rest of the leg seam up to the casings, leaving the openings in each end of the casings. Backstitch to secure. Finish the seams with a zig-zag stitch. Turn and press.

9. Mark the placement of the elastic that will make the gathers to form the doll's bottom.

10. With right sides together, stich body pieces, beginning where indicated on pattern and stitch to first double notch at elastic placement area. Press the seam.

11. Stretch the elastic and pin in place over the seam at the marks. Use a zig-zag stitch to attach the elastic over the seam, keeping it stretched as you sew.

12. Fold down the neck opening 3/8" to make the casing for the cable tie. Go over the seam with a zig-zag stitch for added strength and to prevent fraying.

13. Stitch the rest of the seam up to the casing, leaving the openings at each end. Finish the seam with a zig-zag stitch. Press. Turn body.

Attach the Cloth Parts of the Limbs

See page 62 for step-by-step photos and instructions on attaching the plastic joints.

1. Attach the cloth legs to body by sliding the plastic joint piece into the leg and pushing the spoke of the joint through the clipped reinforced openings on the legs and the body. Put the round washer inside the body, slide onto the spoke, and add the locking piece. (The jointed legs should be able to move freely.)

2. Attach the arms to the body the same way.

Continued on page 48

47

Jointed Body with Partial Vinyl Limbs
Continued from page 47

Make & Insert the Weight Bag

The weight bag gives the body a realistic feel and helps the doll sit on its own. You can use any type of fabric for this bag. I usually use tight woven white cotton. A simple square pouch is all that is needed to hold the pellets that you will use for the weight. Make the pouch just big enough to accommodate the pellets you are using. This weight bag will not "fill" the body, but merely be positioned at the baby's bottom. The size of the weight bag can be adjusted for the weight you want the doll to have. For example, a 3-4-lb. doll feels like a live 6-lb. baby. (Dead weight feels heavier than live weight.)

1. Cut out the appropriate-size weight bag for the amount of pellets or sand you are using your doll.

2. Sew the bag, leaving an opening for filling.

3. Using a funnel, fill the weight bag with plastic pellets or sterilized sand. **(Photo 60)** (If your doll came with bagged plastic pellets, you can re-use these.)

4. Stitch the opening closed.

5. Wrap polyester stuffing around the weight bag. **(Photo 61)**

6. Put some stuffing in the bottom of the body. Insert the wrapped weight bag into the body. **(Photo 62)**

Photo 61 – Placing polyester stuffing around the weight bag.

Photo 60 – Using a funnel to fill the weight bag with plastic pellets.

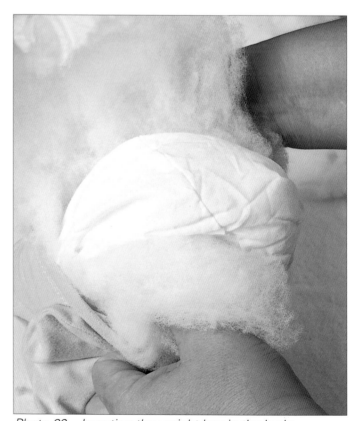

Photo 62 – Inserting the weight bag in the body.

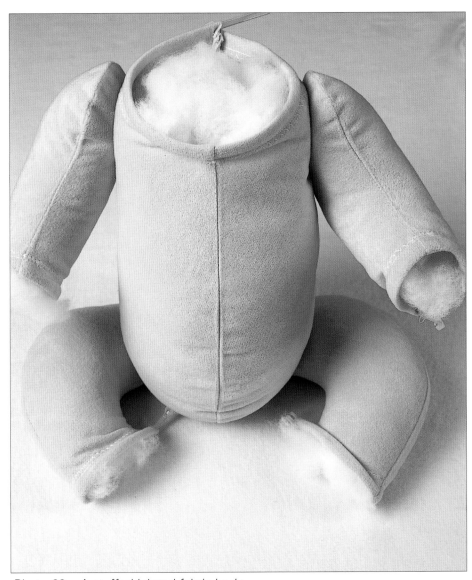

Photo 63 – A stuffed jointed fabric body.

Fill the Cloth Body and Cloth Limbs

1. Add more polyester stuffing to fill the body to the top. (I use about a half bag of stuffing per doll.) Do not overstuff, causing the body to be hard and stiff.

2. Fill the fabric limbs with polyester stuffing. For a pose-able body, stuff loosely. Add more stuffing if you want the body to be stiffer. **(Photo 63)**

Continued on page 50

Jointed Body with Partial Vinyl Limbs
Continued from page 49

Fill the Vinyl Limbs

The vinyl limbs are weighted with plastic pellets and filled with polyester stuffing also.

1. Place the open ends of the vinyl arms and legs on the white felt and trace around them. Cut out the felt circle pieces. These felt pieces will be used to seal the limbs after filling.

2. Pour plastic pellets **(Photo 64)** or sand to within 3/4" of the top of each vinyl limb. Fill the ends of limbs with stuffing.

3. Squeeze some glue around the opening **(Photo 65)** and top with a piece of felt. **(Photo 66)** *Option:* Use silicone sealer instead of glue. **(Photo 67)** Let dry completely. TIP: Place the filled limbs, fabric end down, on a piece of wax paper. The weight of the filler will help to create a tight seal and the glue will not stick to the wax paper.

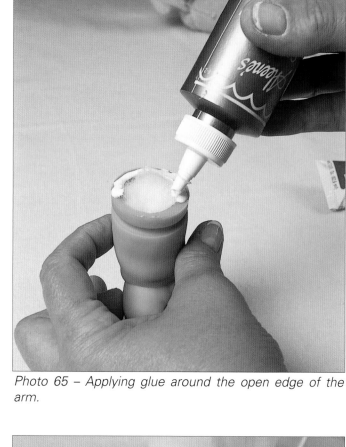

Photo 65 – Applying glue around the open edge of the arm.

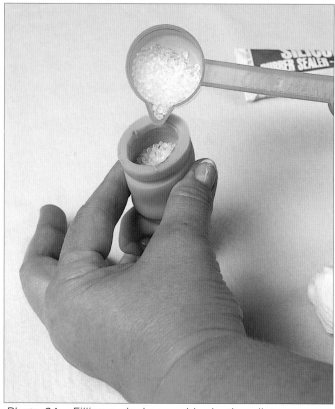

Photo 64 – Filling a vinyl arm with plastic pellets.

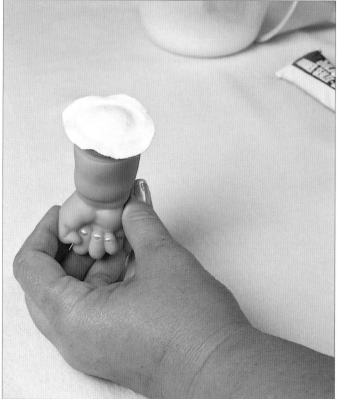

Photo 66 – Sealing the arm opening with a piece of felt.

Attach the Limbs

1. Insert an 8" cable tie in each arm or leg casing in the fabric body and put the end of each cable tie through the loop. **(Photo 59)**

2. Working one limb at a time, slip the fabric limb over the vinyl limb end. **(Photo 68)** Make sure the tie is in the groove of the vinyl limb and secure by pulling the end of the cable tie with needlenose pliers until very tight. **(Photo 69)** Repeat the process to attach both arms and both legs.

3. Trim the ends of the cable ties with wire cutters, cutting with a safe device away from your body. **(Photo 70)** Smooth the cut ends of the cable ties with a metal nail file or emery board. **(Photo 71)** (The sharp edge can be dangerous; smoothing also keeps the doll's clothing from getting snagged.)

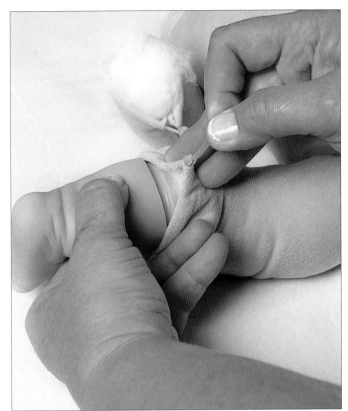

Photo 68 – Placing the fabric limb over a leg. You can see the groove in the leg and the cable tie in the casing.

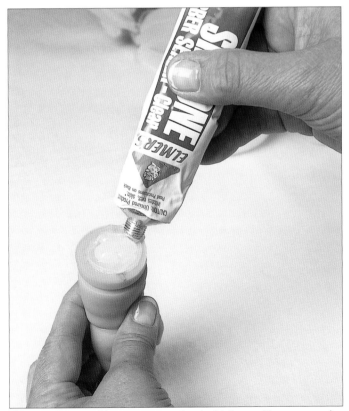

Photo 67 – Alternate method: Using silicone sealer instead of glue.

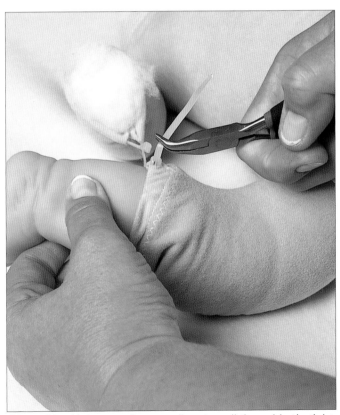

Photo 69 – Using needlenose pliers to pull the cable tie tight.

Continued on page 52

Jointed Body
Continued from page 51

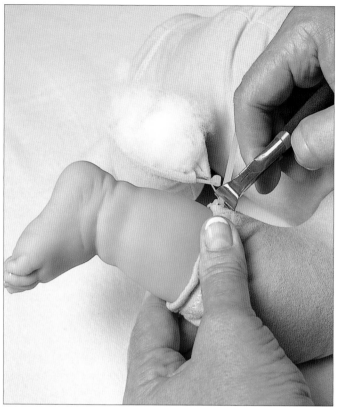

Photo 70 – Using wire cutters to cut off the end of the cable tie.

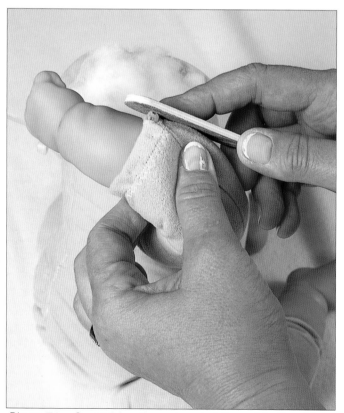

Photo 71 – Smoothing the cut end of the cable tie with an emery board.

Fill & Attach the Head

NOTE: *If you wish your doll to have a pacifier, you will need to attach a magnet inside the head **before*** you fill the head. For information on making pacifiers, see "Making Magnetic Pacifiers."

1. If your doll did not come with a head plug, place the open neck end of the head on a piece of white felt and trace around the bottom opening. Cut out the felt piece. (This will be used to seal the head.)

2. Stuff the head with polyester stuffing. **(Photo 72)** *Option:* Make a small weight bag filled with plastic pellets for the head, following the instructions for making and inserting the weight bag for the body. Surround with polyester stuffing and place inside the head. If you use a weight bag in the head, make sure the head is well-stuffed so the weight bag will stay in place.

3. *Either* replace the head plug that came with the doll **(Photo 73)** *or* glue the round felt piece over the opening of the head to keep the stuffing in place and let the glue dry completely.

4. Insert the 14" cable tie in the neck casing of the cloth body. Put the end of the cable tie through the loop. **(Photo 59)**

5. *Option:* Insert a neck piece, which allows the head to turn freely. Make sure the head is attached inside the neck flange (the groove around the neck piece), and attach the neck piece to the body. **(Photo 73)**

6. Put the head on the body. **(Photo 74)** Position the cable tie in the channel on the doll's neck and use needlenose pliers to pull the cable tie tight, but not so tight that you won't be able to turn the head for posing. **(Photo 75)**

7. Trim the cable tie. Use a nail file or emery board to smooth the cut edges and round the end of the cable tie.

8. Sign the doll's bottom with your nursery name or personal signature, using a fine point permanent marker.

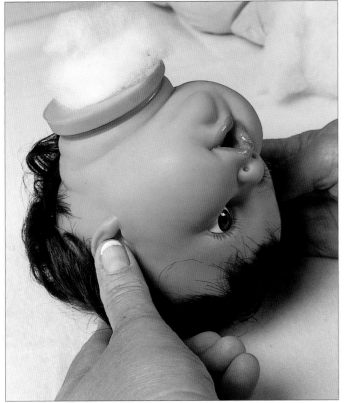

Photo 72 – Stuffing the head with polyester stuffing.

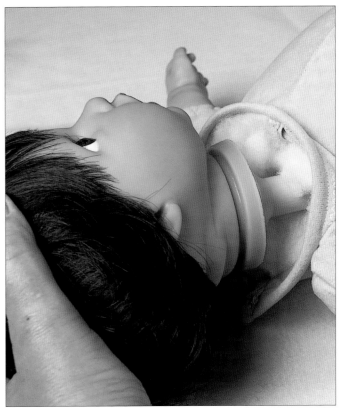

Photo 74 – Placing the head on the body. You can see the cable tie in the neck casing.

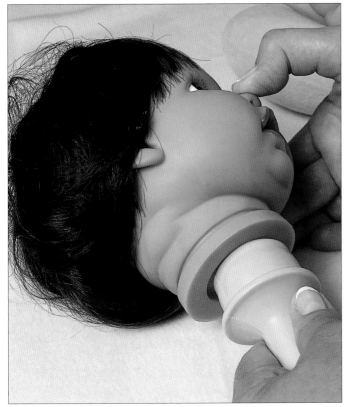

Photo 73 – Attaching the neck piece to the head.

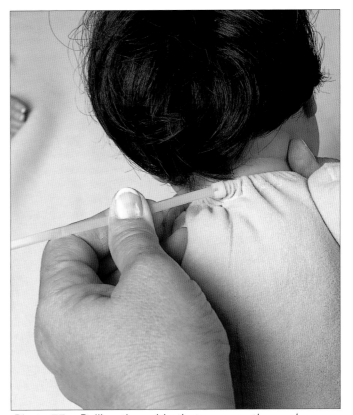

Photo 75 – Pulling the cable tie to secure the neck.

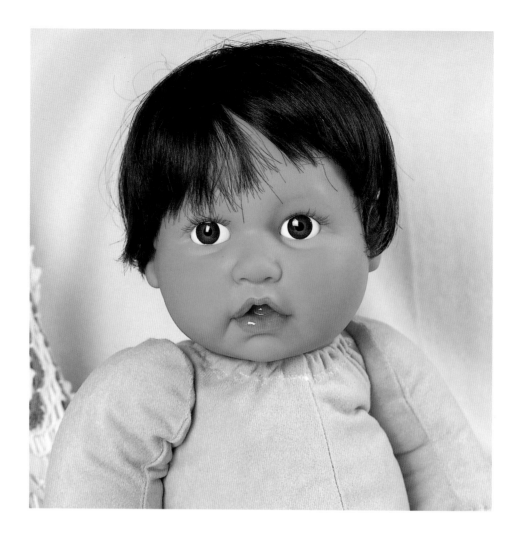

Finished Jointed Limb Body

The doll is now assembled and ready to dress and accessorize. It can sit up and the head, arms, and legs can be rotated for posing.

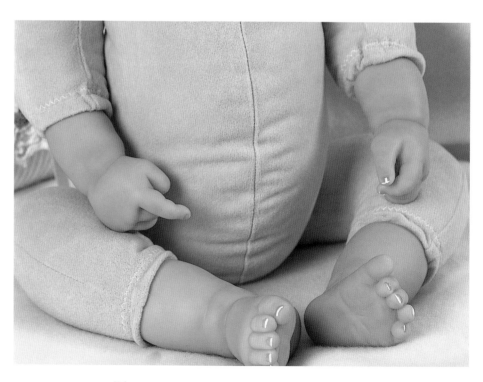

Trunk Style Body

For this easy-to-make body style, you replace a vinyl doll's torso with a soft cloth one and attach the head and full vinyl arms and legs. Like the jointed body, the doll's vinyl arms, legs, and head are attached with cable ties, but this body style does not require doll joints. The ties are attached loosely so the limbs can move freely.

At the back of the book, you'll find body patterns for dolls in a variety of sizes: 20"-21", 17", 14"-15", 14", 9-1/2", and 8". Choose the pattern size that corresponds with the size of your doll.

Supplies Needed

- Doll with vinyl body

- 1/2 yd. white flannel *or* color of your choice (e.g., pink, tan, brown)

- 4" white elastic, 1/8" wide

- Thin plastic cable ties, four 8" and one 12"

- White (or matching color) thread (cotton/polyester blend)

- Bias tape, 1/2" to make casings for the arm, neck, and leg openings (I make my own bias tape, using a quilter's mat and a rotary cutter. I cut 1" strips on the bias, fold them in half, and press.)

- Polyester stuffing

- Tracing paper and pencil

- Transfer paper and tracing wheel

- Scissors

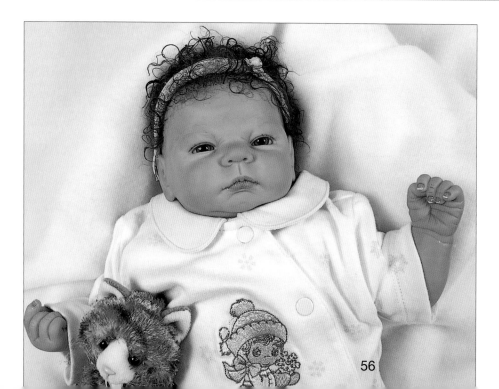

Continued on page 58

Doll pictured left is the made-over doll with trunk-style body and mohair rooted hair. See page 61 showing doll before dressing and styling of hair.

Photo on opposite page shows the made-over doll with a new soft torso and vinyl head and full limbs; at right, the doll before the soft torso and new hair were added.

56

Trunk Style Body
Continued from page 56

Cut & Mark the Pattern

1. Locate the pattern pieces for the size doll you are making. Trace the pattern pieces on tracing paper and cut out.

2. Using the patterns, cut the one front piece (on the fold of the fabric) and the two back pieces from the flannel.

3. Using a tracing wheel and tracing paper, mark the darts. (The darts define the shape of the body.) Mark the placement of the elastic on the back pieces.

Sew

1. Sew all the darts.

2. Sew the two back pieces together.

3. Stretch the elastic to fit the marked area on the back pieces and sew into place.

4. Sew the shoulder seams, side seams, and crotch seam.

5. Attach bias tape to the arm openings, leg openings, and neck opening to make casings for the cable ties. *Option:* For a special touch, add lace around the neck, arm, and leg openings. Place the lace between the bias tape and body and attach as you sew the bias tape.

6. Turn the body inside out and press all the seams. Turn right side out. **(Photo 76, Photo 77)**

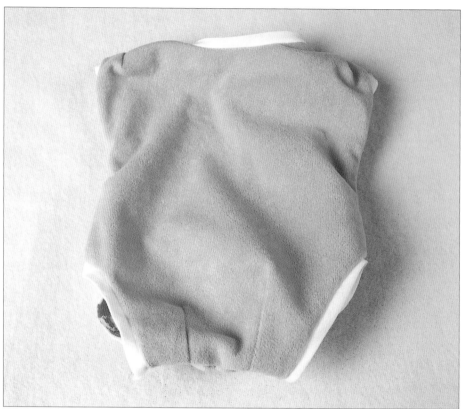
Photo 76 – The trunk style body, front view.

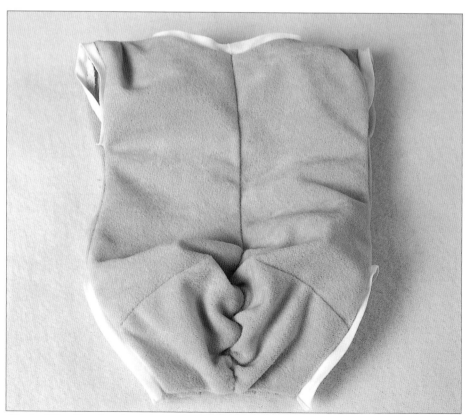
Photo 77 – The trunk style body, back view.

Assemble

1. Insert the 8" cable ties in the arm and leg openings. **(Photo 78)**

2. Working one limb at a time, place the end of the limb inside the opening. Put the end of the cable tie through the loop. Use needlenose pliers to pull the cable tie so the opening fits snugly around the end of the limb. **(Photo 79)** Repeat the process to attach the remaining limbs.

3. Use wire cutters to trim the ends of the cable ties. Smooth the cut ends with an emery board or metal nail file.

4. Stuff the torso with polyester stuffing. **(Photo 80)**

5. To join the body to the head, mark and cut around the neck of the doll. **(Photo 81)** Leave enough space around the neck so the body won't slip off. **(Photo 82)**

6. Insert the 14" cable tie in the neck casing. Place the cut neck piece in the neck opening of the body. Place the end of the cable tie through the loop. Use needlenose pliers to pull the cable tie so the neck opening fits snugly around the neck.

7. Use wire cutters to trim the end of the cable tie. **(Photo 83)** Smooth the cut end with an emery board or metal nail file.

8. Place the doll's head on the neck. ❏

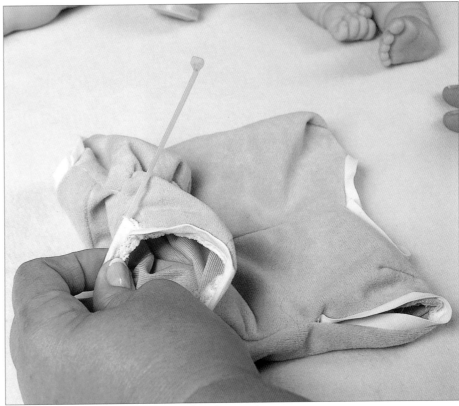

Photo 78 – Inserting a cable tie in a leg casing.

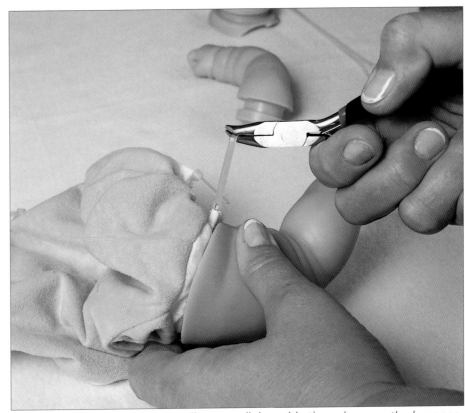

Photo 79 – Using needlenose pliers to pull the cable tie and secure the leg opening to the leg.

Trunk Style Body Assembly
Continued from page 59

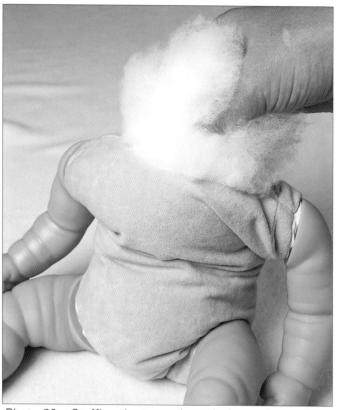

Photo 80 – Stuffing the torso through the neck opening.

Photo 82 – The cut neck piece used to attach the head.

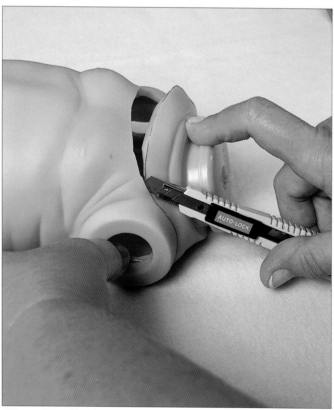

Photo 81 – Cutting around the neck of the original body to make a piece for attaching the head.

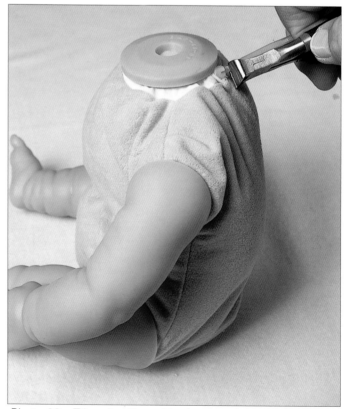

Photo 83 – Trimming the cable tie around the neck opening.

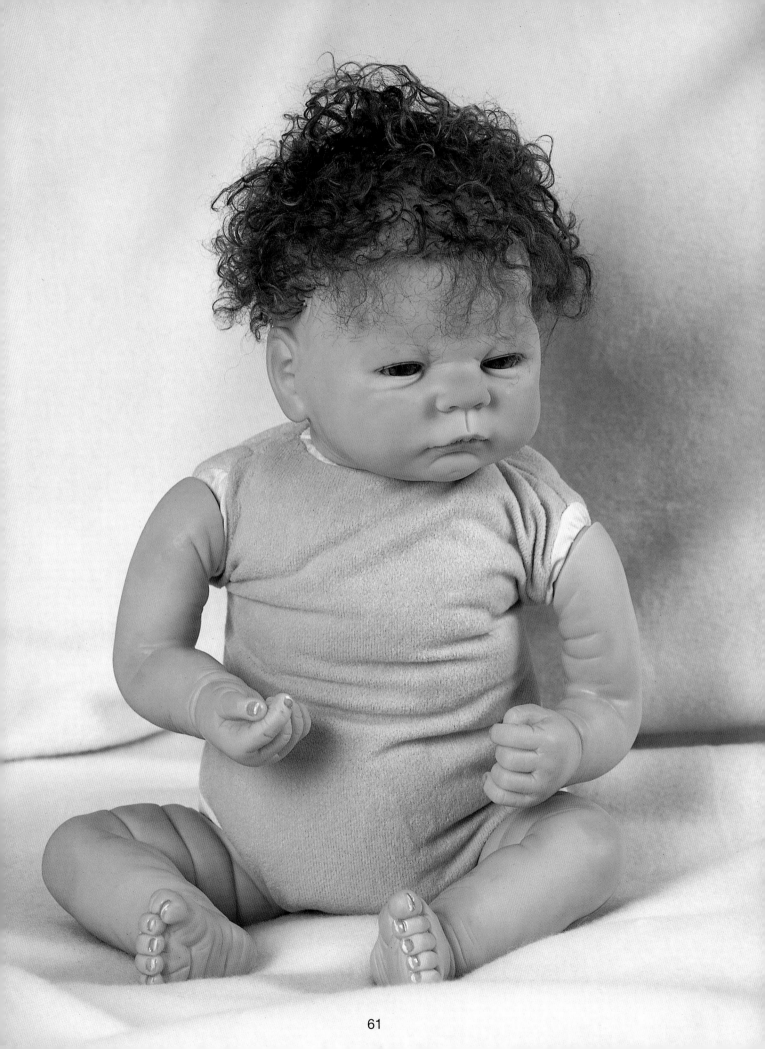

Adding Plastic Joints

Having jointed limbs allows the doll to be positioned more realistically. The photos in this series show how the joint mechanism is inserted.

Joints come in different sizes – larger dolls need larger joints, and the joints for the arms on any particular doll are smaller than the joints for the legs because of the difference in the sizes of the limbs. The joints I use are made of white plastic and allow full rotation of the limb.

Each joint has three pieces: A disc with a spoke in the middle, which is inserted in the leg; a round washer the same size as the disc, which slides onto the spoke inside the torso; and a round locking piece that is smaller than the washer and holds it in place. **(Photo 84)**

To insert the joints, you first need to construct and mark the fabric body, arms, and legs. The joint pieces join the insides of the arms and legs to the outside of the torso. The joint mechanism is concealed inside the body pieces. The areas where the joints are to be inserted have been reinforced with non-woven interfacing for stability. **(Photo 85)**

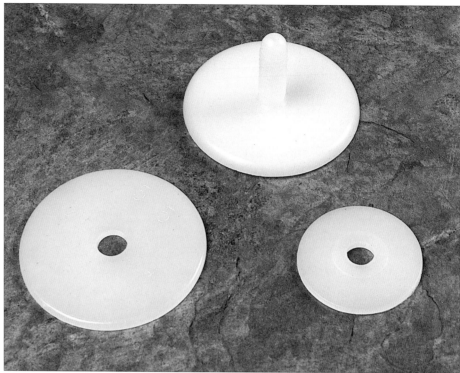

Photo 84 – The parts of a joint. Pictured clockwise from top: Disc with spoke, round washer, locking piece.

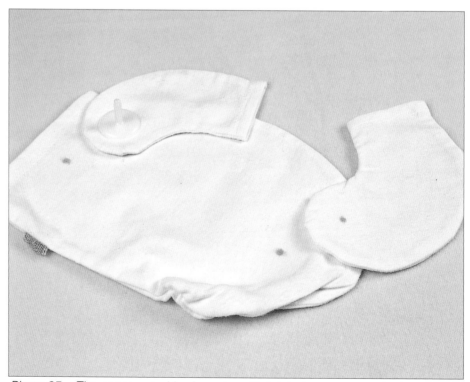

Photo 85 – The constructed body parts with joint placement marked.

The joints are put in place before the torso and limbs are stuffed. They join the inside of the limb to the outside of the torso. Here's how to insert the joints:

1. Use the tips of sharp scissors to clip a small "x" over the marked dots on the reinforced areas of the torso and each limb. **(Photo 86)**

2. Slip the disc with the spoke inside the leg and push the spoke through the clipped hole, pressing the fabric firmly against the joint piece so the spoke is completely exposed. **(Photo 87)**

3. Slip the spoke through the clipped "x" in the torso. **(Photo 88)**

4. Position the round washer inside the torso with the hole in the washer lined up with the spoke. Press the washer firmly against the spoke piece. **(Photo 89)**

5. Slip the locking piece over the spoke **(Photo 90)** and press firmly against the washer. **(Photo 91)** The joint should be able to move freely.

6. Use the same process to attach the other three limbs. ❏

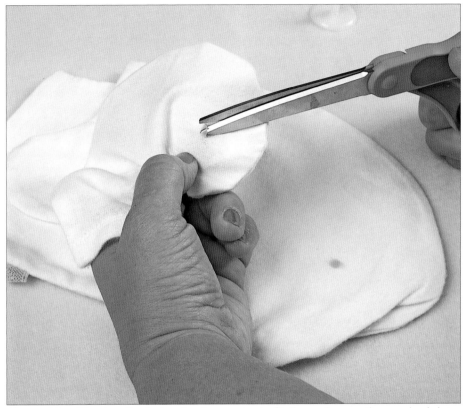

Photo 86 – Clipping the holes for the spoke to fit through over the marked dots.

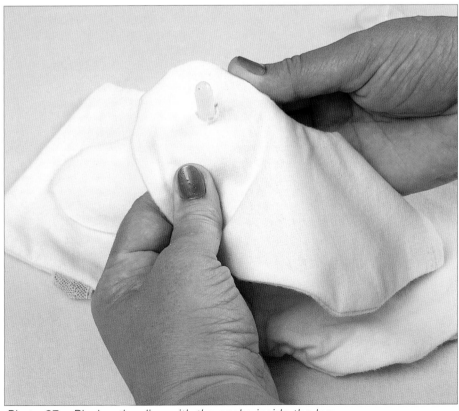

Photo 87 – Placing the disc with the spoke inside the leg.

Photos continued on page 64

Adding Plastic Joints
Continued from page 63

Photo 88 – Slipping the spoke through the clipped hole in the torso.

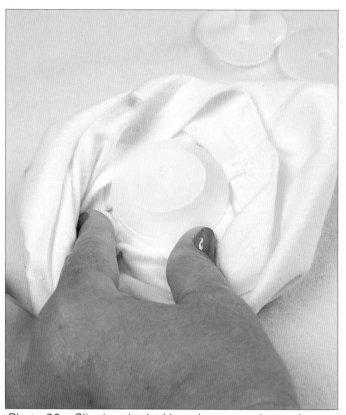

Photo 90 – Slipping the locking piece over the spoke.

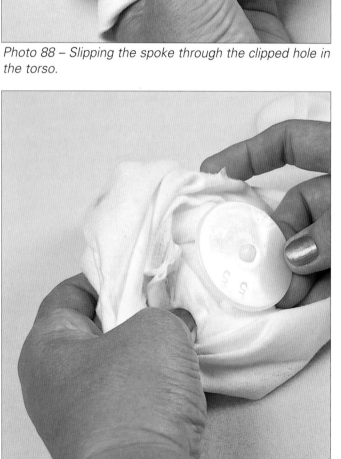

Photo 89 – Positioning the round washer over the spoke inside the torso.

Photo 91 – The locking piece pressed into place.

Doll Accessories

There are a number of things you can make for your doll to make them even more life-like. I have included some of the items I like to make for my dolls

Making Body Plates

You might prefer to have the chest of your doll show for a newborn effect. If you do, you can make a breast plate using part of the vinyl torso that came with your purchased doll.

To make plates, cut and color them according to the following instructions. Lining the body plates with felt (choose a color that matches the doll's skintone) gives the body plates a finished appearance, and the texture of the felt helps keep the plates in place on the cloth body. The detachable plates can be laid on the cloth body for photographs or attached to the cloth body with ribbon ties for display, allowing you to open some of the clothes to show parts of the torso.

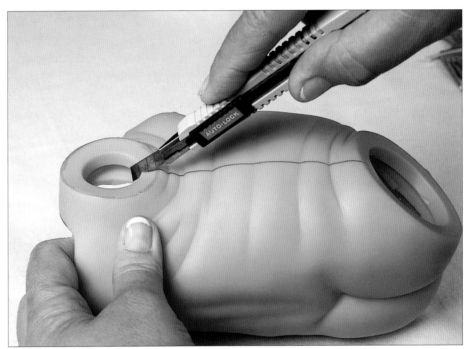

Photo 92 – Cutting the vinyl torso into two pieces.

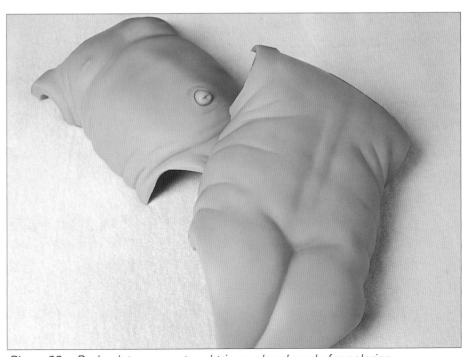

Photo 93 – Body plates are cut and trimmed and ready for coloring.

Making Body Plates
Continued from page 65

Here's how:

1. Warm the vinyl body in hot water to make cutting easier. Cut the torso into two pieces, a front and a back, using a craft knife. Cut down the sides, across the shoulders, and across the crotch area. **(Photo 92)**

2. Use your craft knife to remove the excess vinyl around the areas where the arms and legs join the torso. Carefully round the edges at the shoulders and the crotch. **(Photo 93)** TIP: Cut the thick sections of the vinyl at an angle for a look that's more pleasing to the eye.

3. Dye and color the plates, following the same procedure and using the same colors you used for the limbs and head to ensure an exact match.

4. Add blushing to the outsides of the plates if you used blushing on the other vinyl parts.

5. Use a leather punch to make holes around the edges of the pieces for the ties. *Option:* Place the ribbon between the body plate and the felt lining (see the next step) before you glue the felt in place.

6. Cut pieces of felt to line the insides of the body plates. Glue the felt pieces to the plates with white craft glue. Let dry overnight. If you punched holes in the body plates, use a craft knife to cut out the felt behind the holes.

7. Position the plate on the doll's torso and mark the placement of the holes with a disappearing marker. Cut pieces of ribbon and loop the ribbon through the holes in the breast plate.

8. You can attach the plate to the body in one of several ways:

   1) Sew the ends of each ribbon piece to the cloth body.

   2) Sew snaps to the ends of the ribbon pieces looped to the vinyl body and sew the matching snap pieces to the proper position on the cloth body.

   3) Sew matching pieces of ribbon to marked positions on the cloth body so that the plate can be tied to the cloth body. ❏

A Birth Certificate for Your Doll

Art for certificates are available from stores that sell printed papers and also online. It can include the doll's name and statistics like the length, weight, and date and place of "birth." The most important information is the name of the doll's creator – YOU!

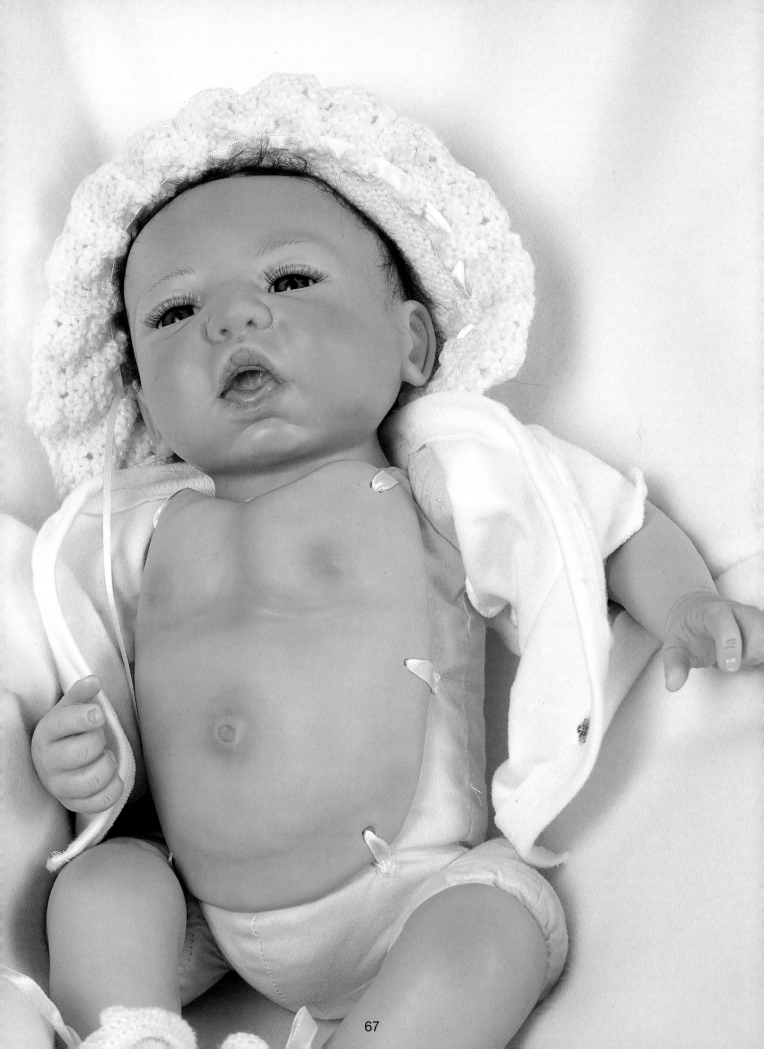

Making Magnetic Pacifiers

You can create a pacifier as an accessory for your doll by modifying a regular baby pacifier. Pacifiers can be purchased at dollar stores or department stores. Look for a pacifier with a unique color or design – perhaps one that will match the outfit the doll will be wearing. I have seen cute pacifiers with yarn wrapped around them and added lace and trim.

A magnet is attached to the pacifier so it will stay in or on the dolls mouth. A pair of magnets – one inside the doll's head and one on the pacifier – holds the pacifier in place. The magnets I use for pacifiers are earth magnets (neodymium or NdFeB magnets, 3/8" in diameter and about 1/8". You can find them online). You'll also need some strong multi-purpose adhesive to glue the magnets in place.

To use a pacifier with your doll, the doll needs to have a mouth that will accommodate a pacifier or that would look natural with a pacifier on the mouth.

Here's how:

1. Mark the inside and outside magnets so you'll be able to tell which sides should face each other for positioning.

2. Use scissors to cut off the top of the nipple end of the pacifier, cutting straight across and leaving a little of the nipple on the pacifier. **(Photo 94)** TIP: If the pacifier is very curved, you'll want to leave more of the nipple. **See Photo 96.**

3. Use some strong multi-purpose clear glue to attach the outside magnet to the pacifier inside what remains of the nipple. **(Photo 95)** Note the mark on the magnet that shows which side should be toward the doll's face. Let dry 24 hours.

4. Position the other (inside) magnet inside the doll's head behind the mouth, using the mark on the magnet to choose the side that needs to be towards the outside.

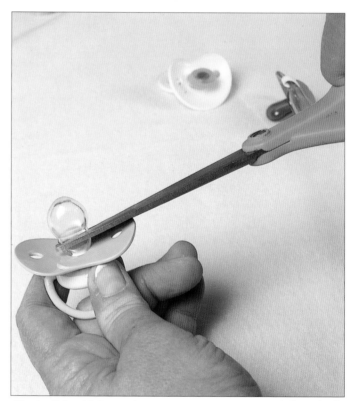

Photo 94 – Using scissors to remove most of the nipple from the pacifier.

5. Glue the inside magnet in place. Place the pacifier with the outside magnet over the mouth – it will hold the inside magnet in place until the glue dries. Let set for 24 hours.

CAUTION: These magnets work great but they **must** be kept away from people who wear pacemakers and away from computers and other items that are magnet-sensitive.

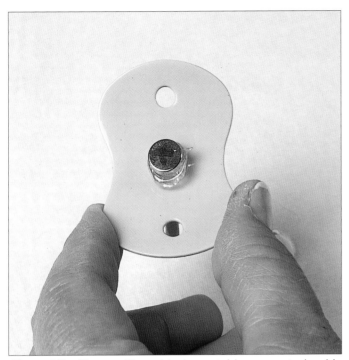

Photo 95 – The pacifier with the outside magnet glued in place.

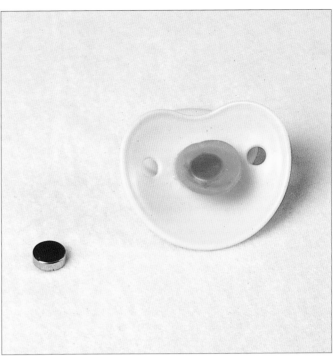

Photo 96 – A completed pacifier. Because this one is curvier, more of the nipple was left in place.

Making Baby Bottles

You can make a bottle filled with faux formula to accessorize your doll. For a realistic look, use some off-white fabric softener to make faux formula. (Fabric softener that's off-white, rather than pure white in color, looks more like formula.) NOTE: I seal the nipple of the bottle and glue it and the lid in place to ensure small children will not be able to try to drink the contents or open the bottle.

Here's how:

1. Combine 1/2 cup off-white fabric softener and 1/2 cup water. Mix well.

2. Place the mixture in a 4-ounce baby plastic bottle.

3. Fill the nipple of the bottle with clear silicone. Allow to dry.

4. Glue the nipple to the top to the bottle.

5. Place glue on the threads of the screw ring top and screw in place. Let dry. ❑

Finishing the Doll

Your doll is now complete – all that's left is to select some clothing (you'll find numerous examples in the sections titled "Jan's Nursery" and "Gallery of Dolls") and dress the doll.

Real baby clothes will fit these dolls. Preemie and newborn sizes fit the appropriate size dolls. Three month size fits the larger dolls.

Congratulations on the new addition to your family.

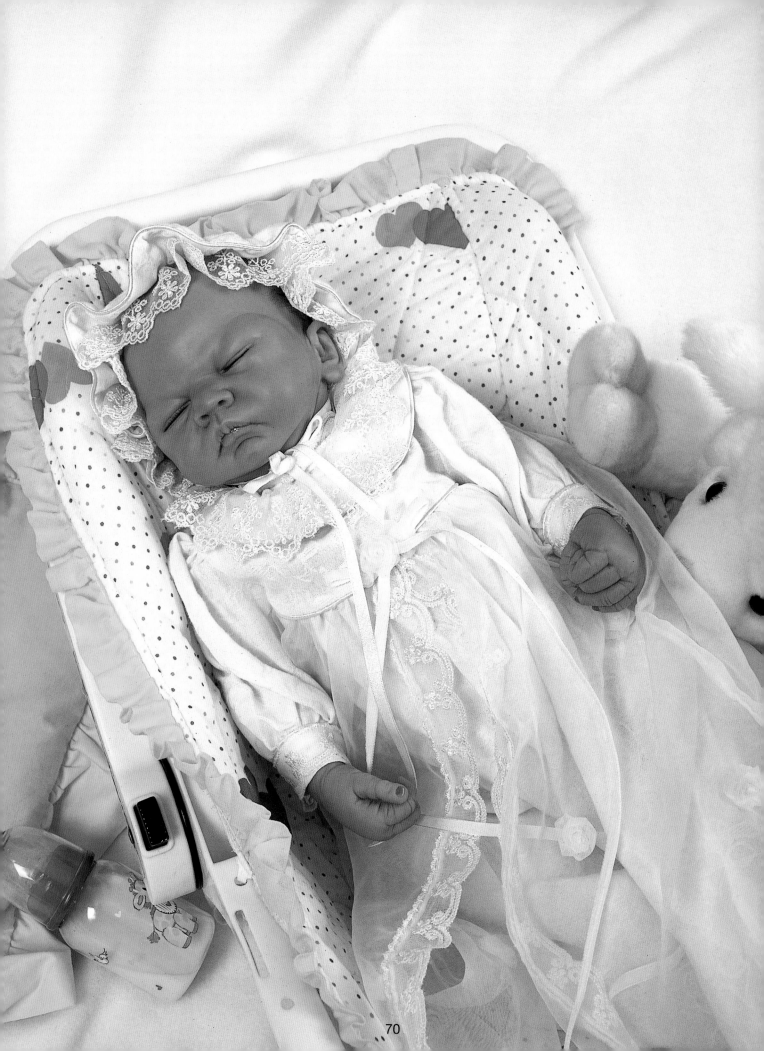

Jan's Nursery

In this section are two dozen examples of doll makeovers. They have been dressed, posed, and accessorized for the photographs, just as real babies might be. Looking at their pictures, it's easy to see how appealing they are and how life-like they look. The individual characteristics – the personality, if you will – of each doll creation is evident.

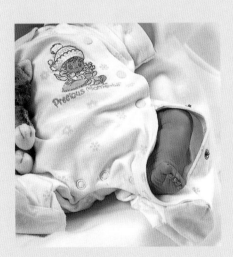

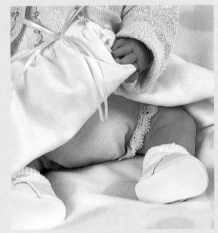

Baby Grace

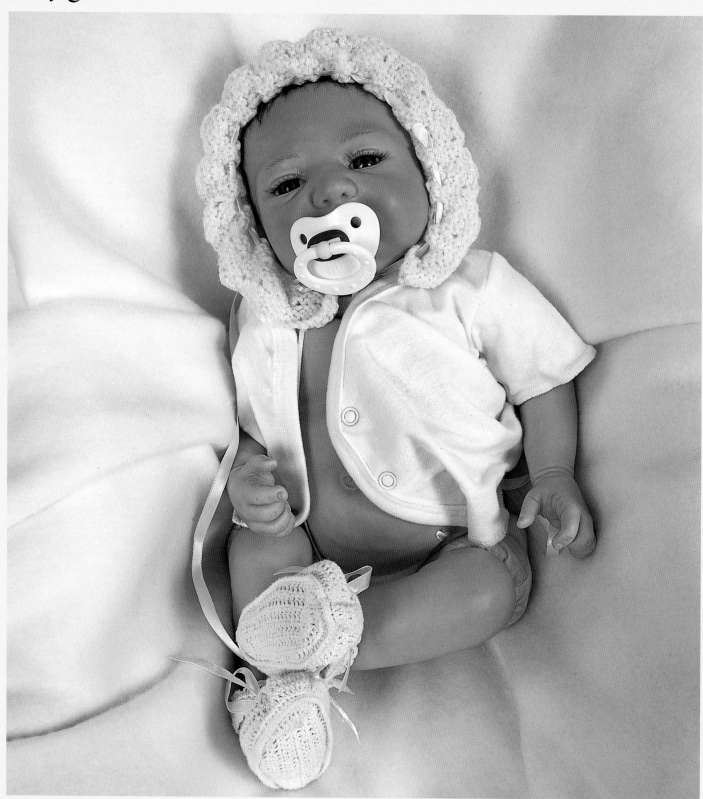

Doll Size: Preemie
Body Type: Jointed cloth body with vinyl limbs and body plates

She came with a silicone body. Part of the body was used to make the body plate. Baby Grace is dressed all in white and has a magnetic pacifier to match. Her curly hair is hand rooted mohair. Her booties and bonnet are hand knit. She wears a preemie size undershirt that allows her chest to show. See "Doll Accessories" section for how to make body plate and pacifier.

Ricci Sue

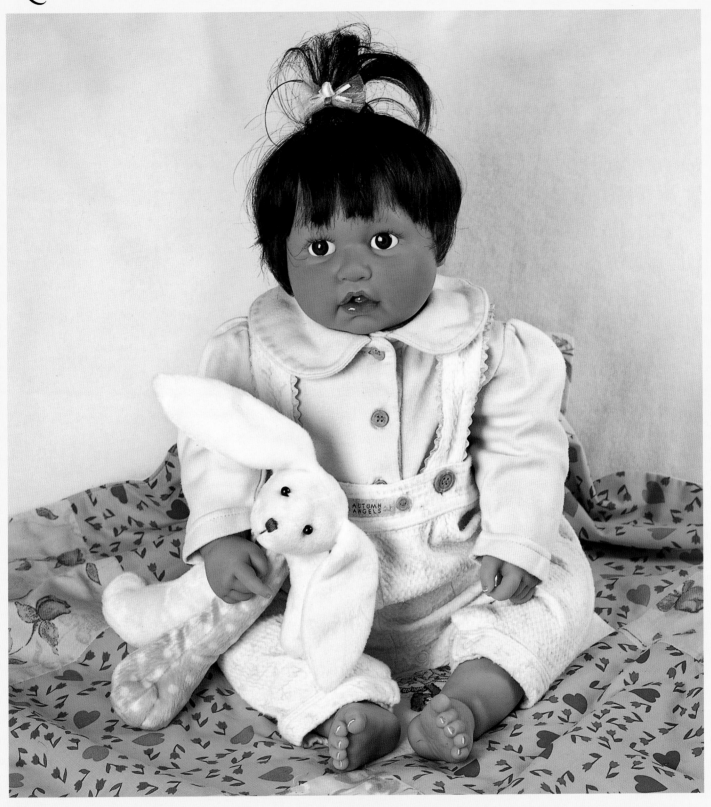

Doll Size: 20" newborn
Body Type: Jointed with partial vinyl limbs

Ricci Sue's glossy brown hair is a wig chosen to match her brown eyes and long brown eyelashes, which were applied in a strip. Her pink glossy lip color is just a bit darker than her pastel pink shirt and the trim on her overalls. A white ribbon rose adorns the bow clipped in her hair, and she's holding a pink-and-white stuffed rabbit. She wears 3-month size clothing.

Jayden

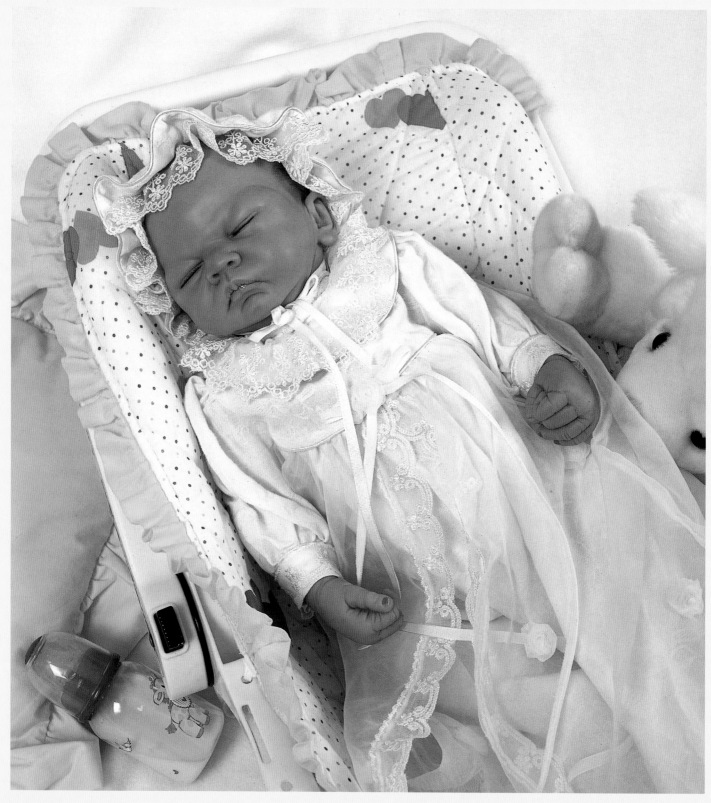

Doll Size: 20" newborn
Doll Size: Newborn
Body Type: Silicone body

Jayden is a sleeping doll. She wears a long lacy dress and a matching bonnet. Her dark curly hair and eyelashes were hand rooted. The baby bottle contains faux formula. See "Doll Accessories" chapter for making baby bottle.

Debra Lynn

Doll Size: Newborn
Body Type: Jointed

Debra has big brown eyes, long curly eyelashes, and a dark brown mohair wig. Feminine touches include yellow satin rosebuds on her hair ribbon and around her neck, a ribbon belt with a bow, and lace ruffles on her sleeves.

75

Corbin Dean

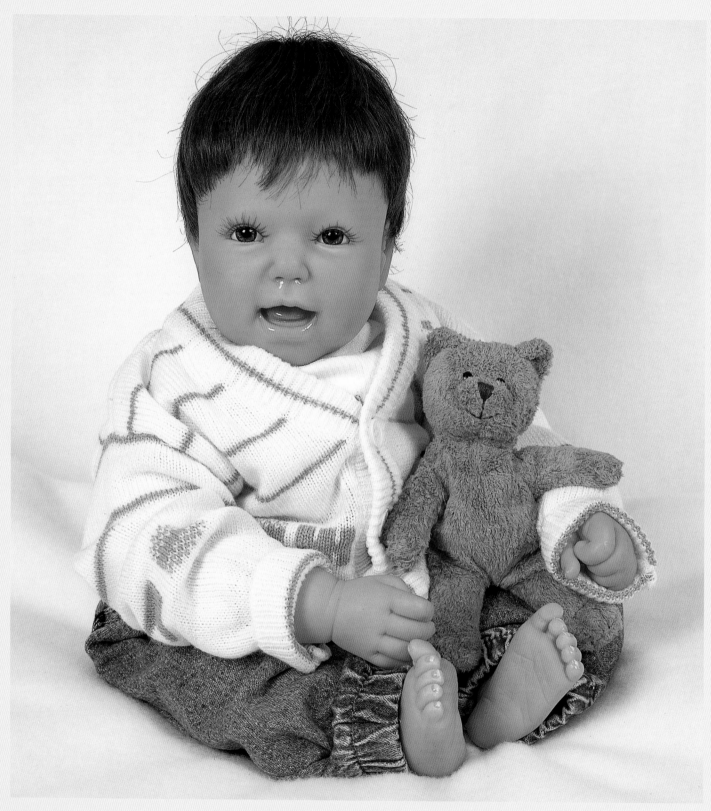

Doll Size: Preemie
Body Type: Jointed

Mischievous-looking Corbin Dean hugs a tiny teddy bear. His silky dark hair is a wig. The "wet nose" effect above his upper lip was achieved by judicious application of super gloss varnish or clear glaze.

Joshua John

Doll Size: Preemie
Body Type: Jointed

Smiling Joshua has new eyes and eyelashes but wears his original vinyl hair color. His skin is dyed and rouged. Preemie baby clothes fit him well.

Abigail Nicole

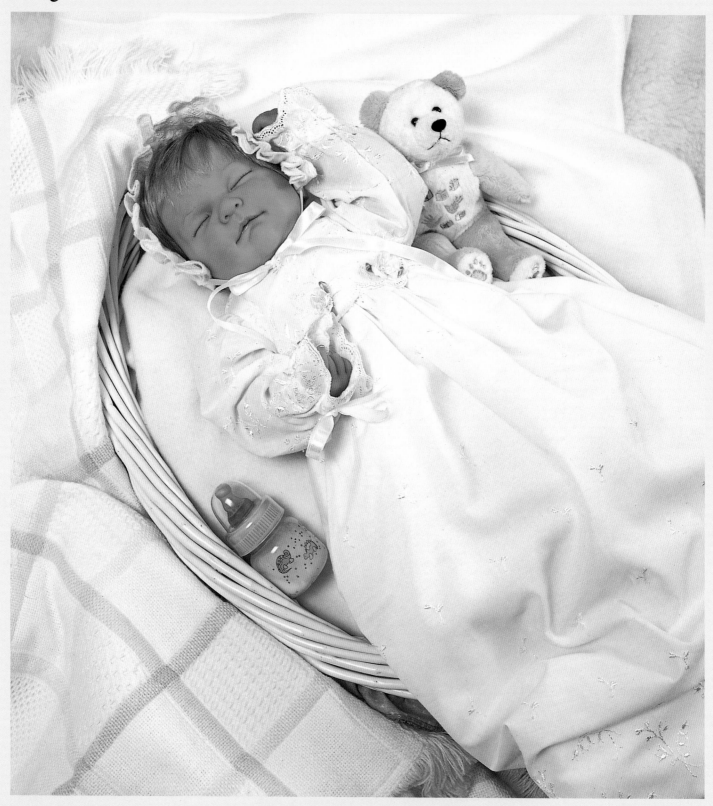

Doll Size: Newborn
Body Type: Jointed

Sleeping Abigail Nicole is posed realistically in her basket crib with one arm raised to her face. She wears a blonde wig and has hand rooted eyelashes. Crib accessories include stuffed animals and a decorated baby bottle with faux formula. To make the faux formula in bottle, see "Making Baby Bottles" in the Making Accessories section.

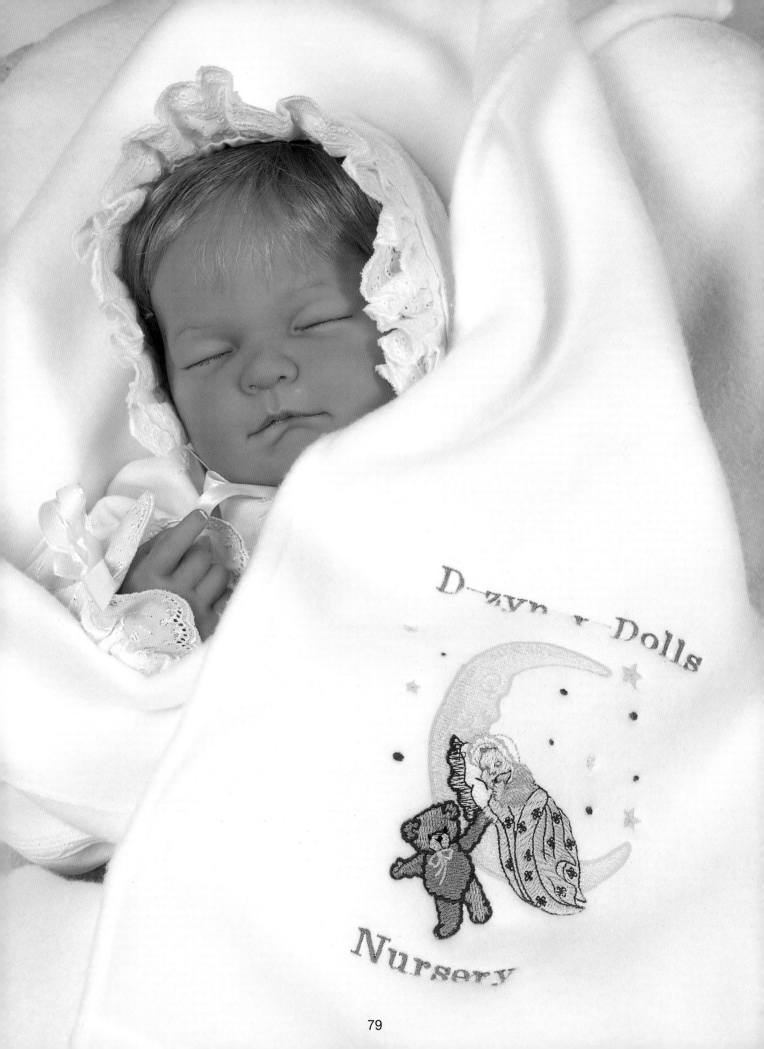

Camey Jo

Doll Size: 17" Preemie
Body Type: Jointed with full vinyl legs and partial vinyl arms

Camey Jo has a brown wig and wide-open brown eyes framed by feathery long eyelashes. Her pouty, rosy lips are accentuated by her pink clothes and the eyelet-ruffled pink liner of her carrier basket.

Ryan Theodore

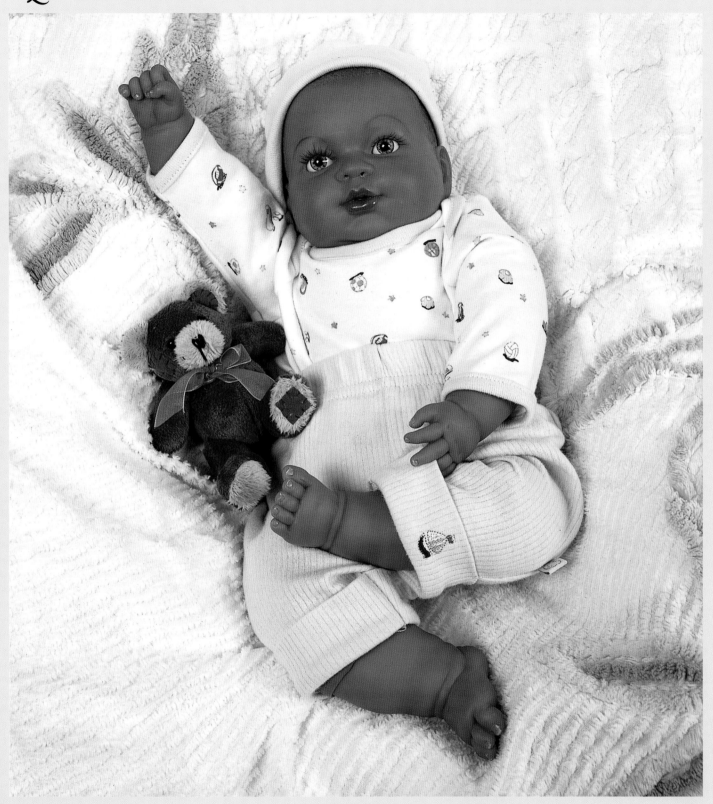

Doll Size: Preemie
Body Type: Soft jointed

Ryan's extended arm and crossed leg suggest activity, and his blue pants and sports-motif t-shirt leave no doubt that he's a boy. He has vinyl hair, green eyes, and long, thick eyelashes. He's posed on a chenille blanket with his tiny teddy tucked next to his body.

Becky

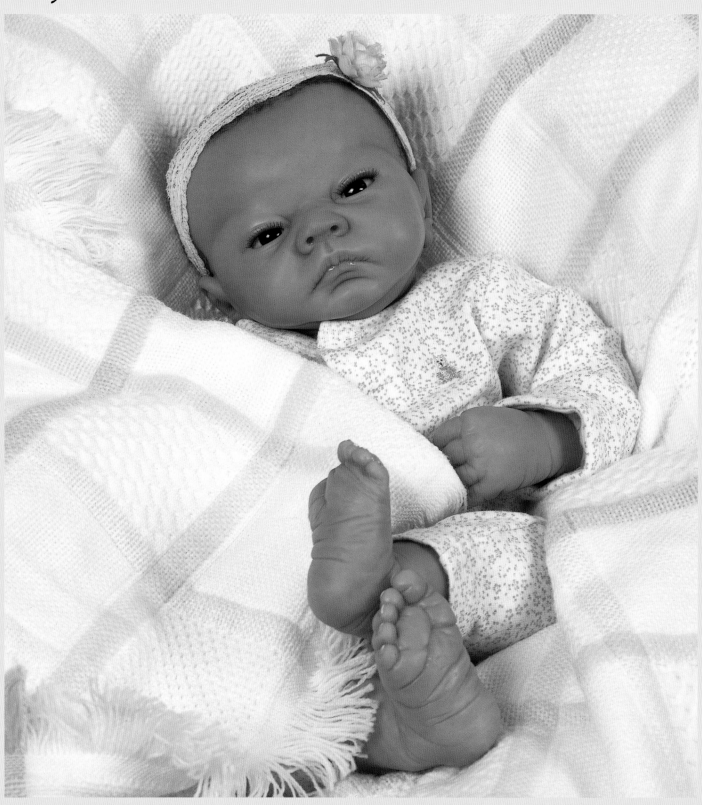

Doll Size: Newborn
Body Type: Jointed silicone body with partial limbs

A cap with a pink rosebud covers Becky's hand rooted mohair hair. Blushing gives her skin a realistic appearance; her lips have just a touch of color and shine.

Heidi Jo

Doll Size: Toddler
(3-6 months)
Body Type: Jointed with
partial limbs

Heidi Jo's bright blue eyes are framed with thick eyelashes. Her silky straight dark hair is a wig. Her "sucky" bottom lip gives her an intense expression. She wears a frilly pink dress and cap with crocheted booties, and sits in a white wicker chair.

Scotty

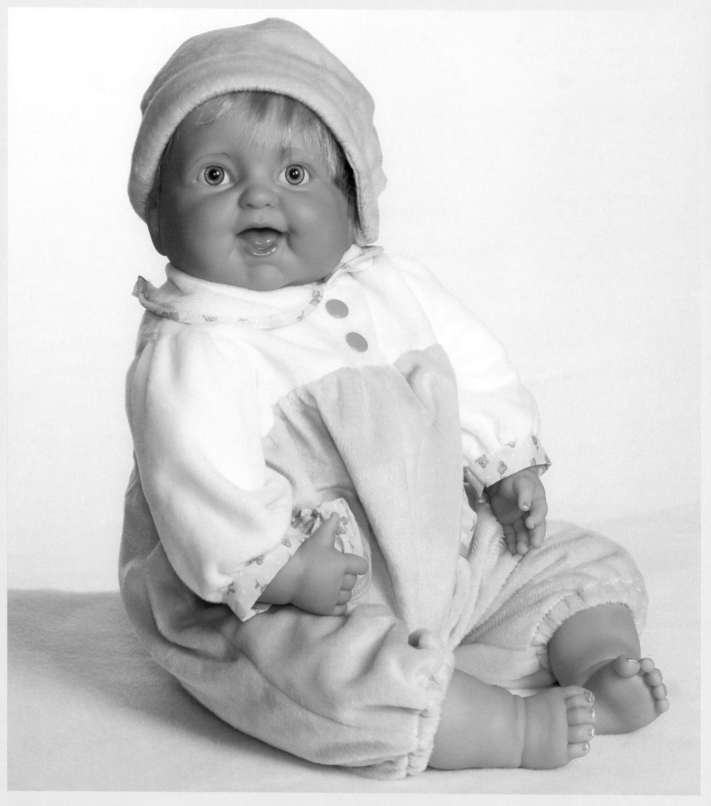

Doll Size: Preemie
Body Type: Jointed

Scotty's blond wig peeks out from under his blue cap, which accentuates his wide blue eyes. His cheeks show subtle blushing and his lips and open mouth have a wet look.

Taylor Calvin

Doll Size: Newborn
Body Type: Full vinyl limbs

Taylor wears a green outfit that includes a cap over a shiny blonde wig. Baby eyelashes frame new brown eyes. Notice the blushing and veining that give the skin such a realistic look.

Suzanna

Doll Size: Toddler
(3-6 months)
Body Type: Jointed with
partial limbs

A ruffled bonnet covers the shiny brown wig and frames Suzanna's face, which has full cheeks, deep blue eyes, and a "sucky" bottom lip. Her dress and pantaloons are trimmed with pink satin ribbons, and she wears pink and white crocheted booties.

Sydney

Doll Size: Preemie
Body Type: Jointed silicone with partial limbs

Sydney looks like she's been dressed up for her first official photograph. This little princess wears a pearl-and-rosebud "ribbon" around her head. Her curly hair is hand rooted mohair, her eyes are blue, and her pink-tinted lips glisten.

James Daniel

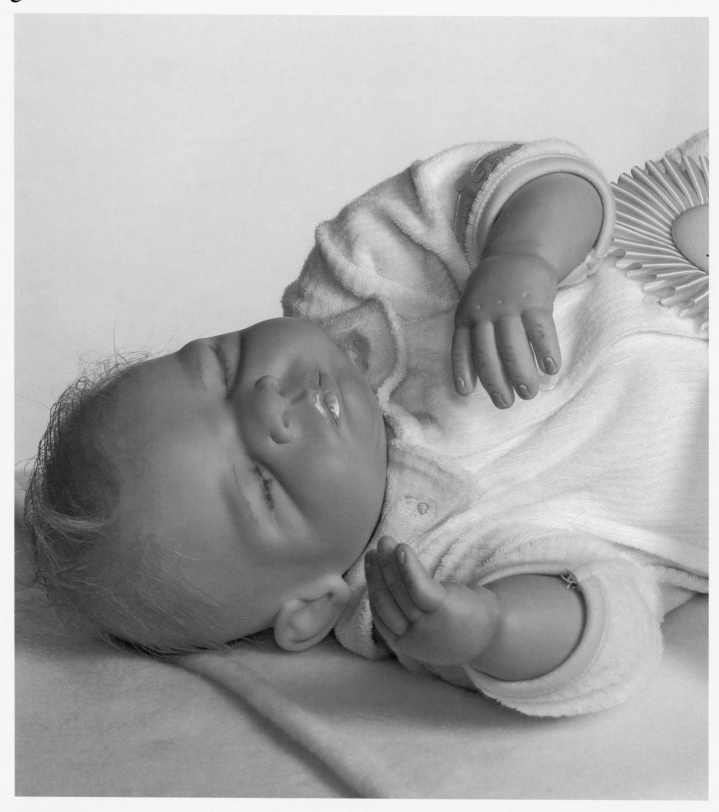

Doll Size: Newborn
Body Type: Jointed

This sleeping baby is a prize winner. He has hand rooted light hair and eyelashes and realistic blushing on his face and hands. His lips have a wet look.

Earl Jonathan

Doll Size: Newborn
Body Type: Jointed

Sleeping Earl Jonathan is positioned on his side in a realistic pose. He has hand rooted mohair eyelashes and hair. His one-piece pajamas have animal feet and he wears a soft knitted cap.

Olivia

Doll Size: 17" Preemie
Body Type: Jointed with full vinyl legs and partial vinyl arms

Olivia has full, colored lips, blushed cheeks, deep brown eyes, and a brown wig. Her lace-trimmed dress, face-framing bonnet, and white leggings were hand-knitted.

Amy Jo

Doll Size: Preemie
Body Type: Jointed with partial vinyl limbs

Amy Jo wears a serious expression and white clothes with pink accents. Her lips are barely pink, her eyes are deep blue, and she has hand rooted hair.

Baby Emma Danae

Doll Size: 14"
Body Type: Trunk style body with full vinyl limbs. Lace trim has been put around arm and leg openings of cloth body to dress it up.

Emma has deep blue eyes, long eyelashes, and shiny tinted lips. Part of her thick platinum blonde hair (a curly wig) is caught up in a flower-trimmed white grosgrain bow. She wears a collared dress, a pink sweater, and white shoes.

Jody Marie

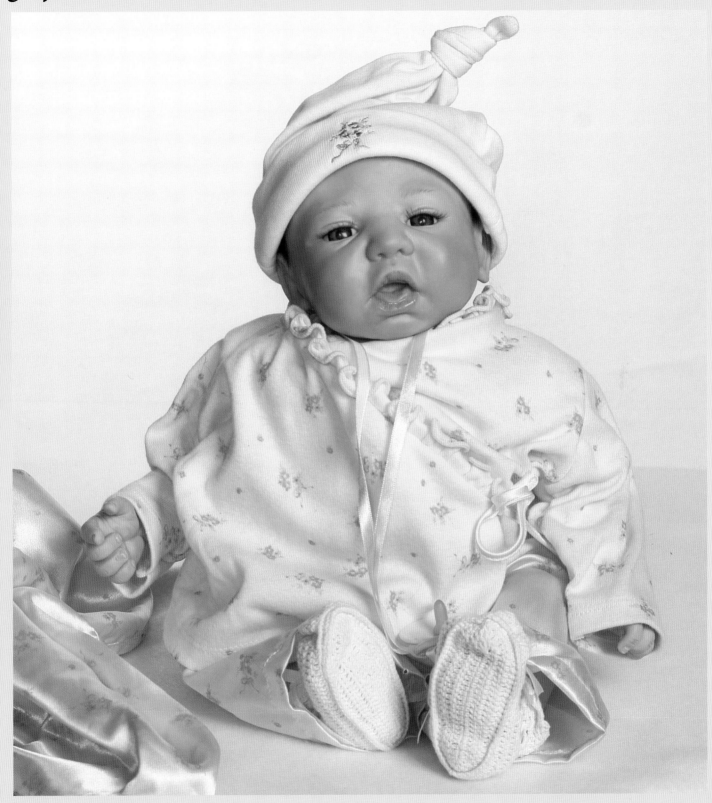

Doll Size: Preemie
Body Type: Jointed with full vinyl limbs and body plate

Jody Marie is shown in a pink satin outfit with a matching blanket. A pink-and-white knitted cap covers her hand rooted hair. Her cheeks are blushed and her lips and mouth are faintly tinted. Her kimona can be opened to display her vinyl chest.

Jacy Bryn

Doll Size: 14"
Body Type: Trunk style body with full vinyl limbs. Lace trim has been put around arm and leg openings of cloth body to dress it up.

Jacy's ready for a garden party in her flowered summer frock and t-strap shoes. Her new eyes are deep aquamarine and her lips glisten with color. A coordinating ribbon is tied in a bow around her shiny straight blonde hair wig.

95

Heather Dawn

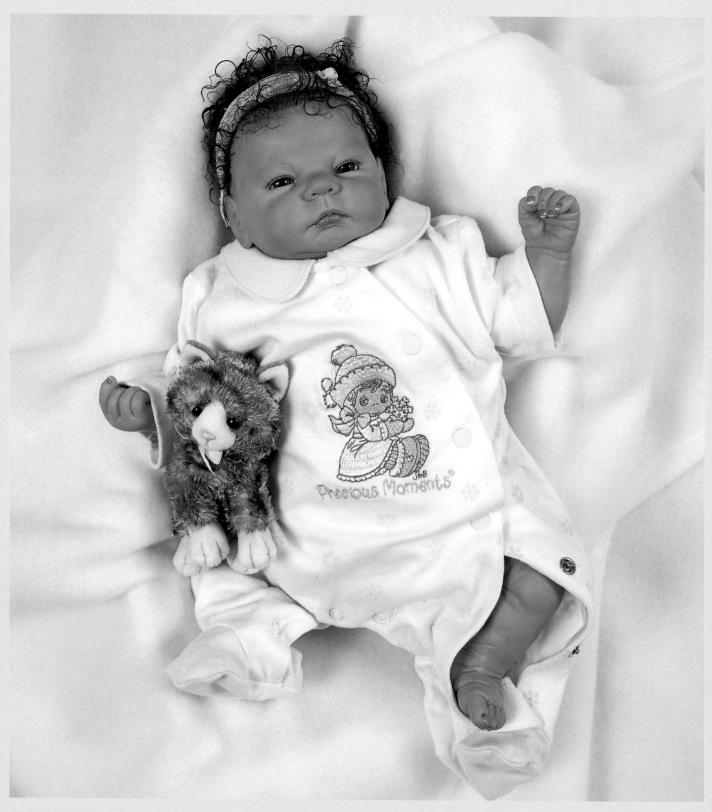

Doll Size: 14" preemie
Body Type: Trunk style body with full vinyl limbs

Heather has a head full of hand-rooted curly mohair. Because she's a preemie, it's only natural that her clothes are a little too big for her body. And, of course, she's too young to sit up.

Payton Thomas

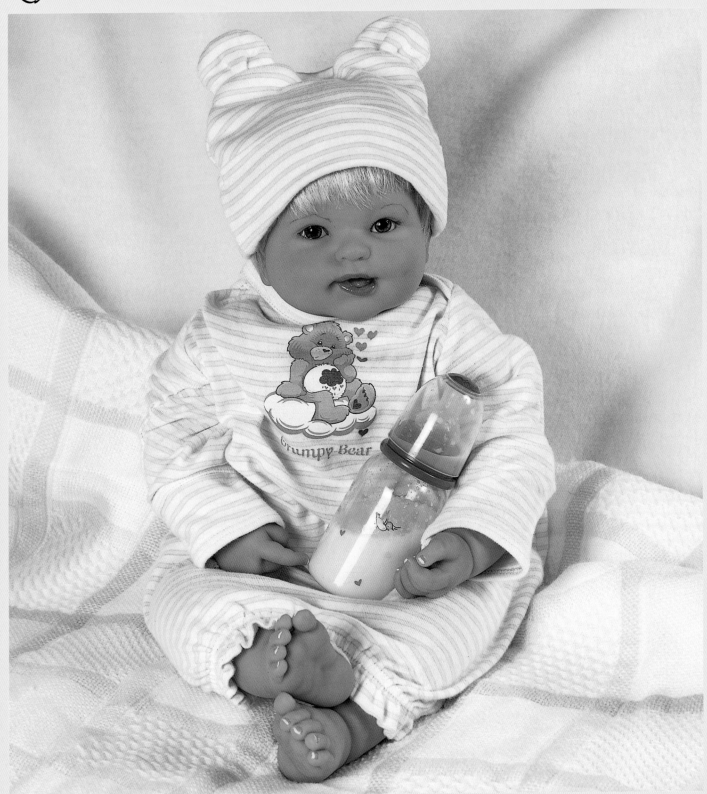

Doll Size: Newborn
Body Type: Jointed with partial vinyl limbs

Payton Thomas's straight blond hair (a modacrylic wig) peeks out from under a white stocking cap. He has deep blue eyes, and his mouth was finished with glossy varnish for a wet look. He's holding a bottle that contains fake formula. (See "Making Baby Bottles.")

Body Patterns

In this section you'll find the patterns for making doll bodies in a range of sizes. You may modify the patterns for a shorter or longer body by adding or subtracting length from the middle of the body.

When sewing bodies, I use a straight stitch on all seams and finish the seams with a zig zag stitch. This secures the seam, and makes it stronger and less likely to fray. The seam allowance for all the patterns is 1/4".

Dart

20"-21" Body Back
For dolls with full vinyl limbs

Cut two

Enlarge pattern 120% for actual size

Place elastic here for gathers

Dart

Trunk-style Body #1
You will need a front and back pattern piece for this style body.

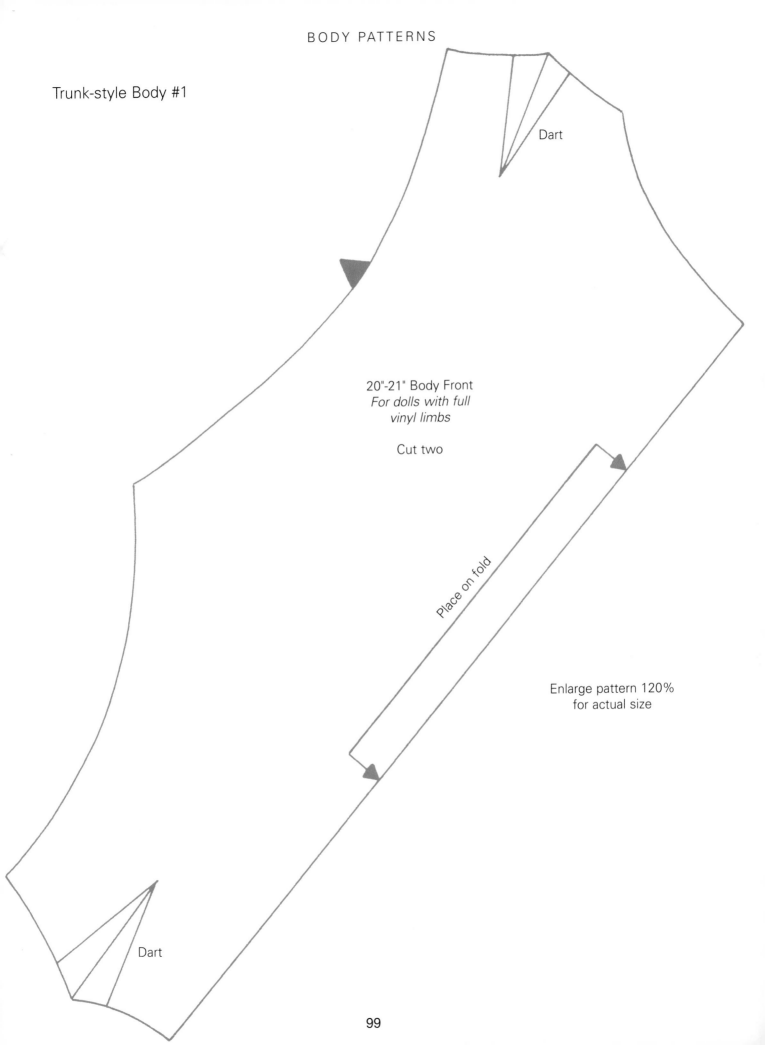

Trunk-style Body #1

Dart

20"-21" Body Front
For dolls with full vinyl limbs

Cut two

Place on fold

Enlarge pattern 120%
for actual size

Dart

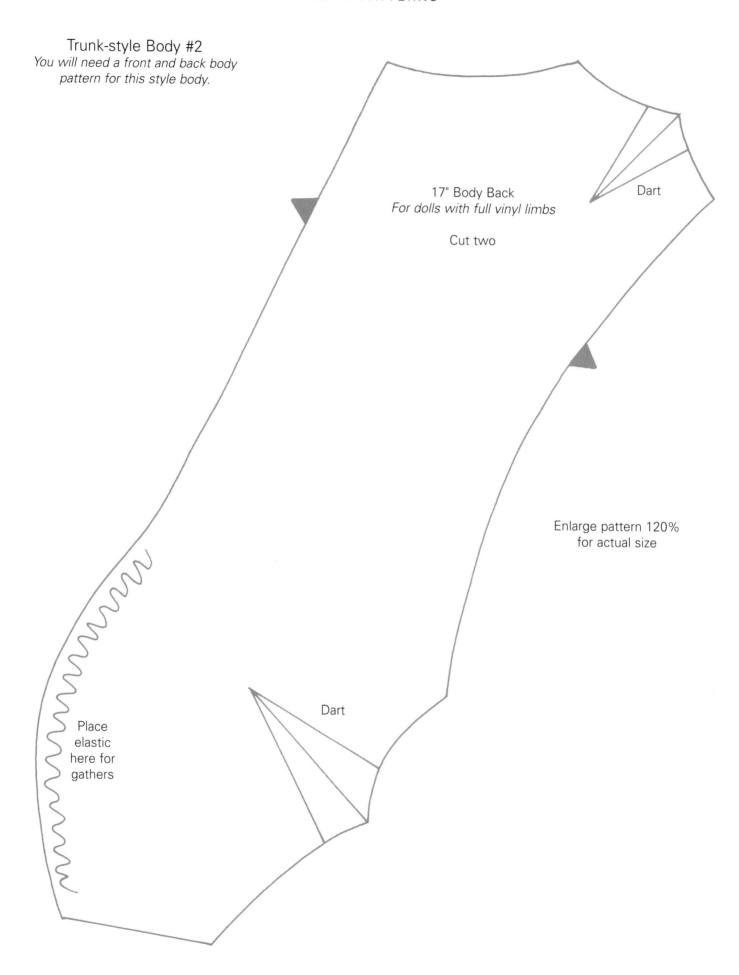

Trunk-style Body #2
You will need a front and back body pattern for this style body.

17" Body Back
For dolls with full vinyl limbs

Cut two

Dart

Enlarge pattern 120%
for actual size

Dart

Place
elastic
here for
gathers

Trunk-style Body #2

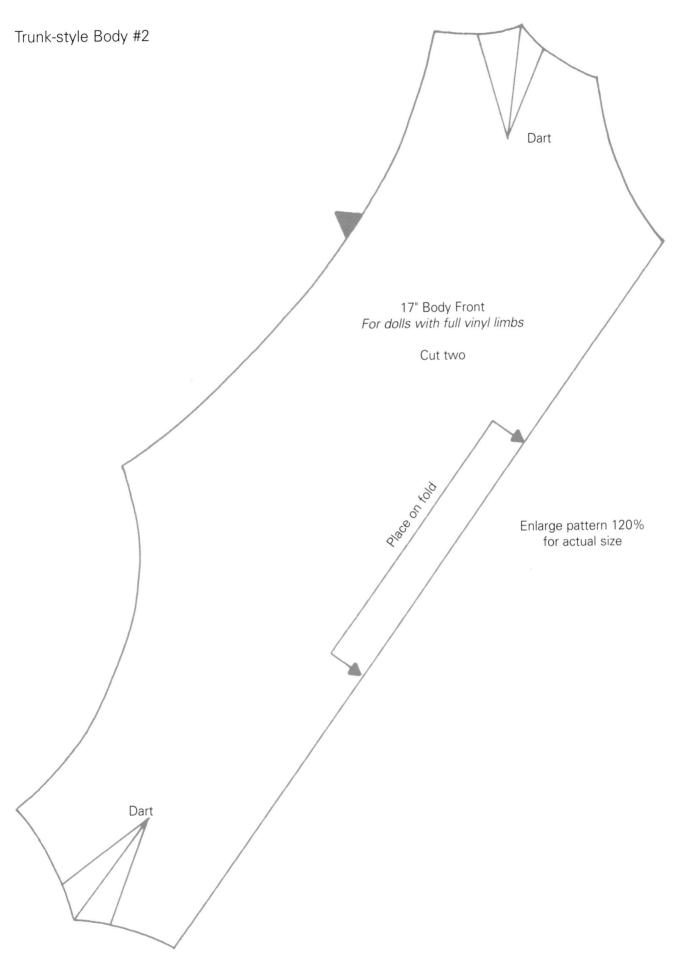

Dart

17" Body Front
For dolls with full vinyl limbs

Cut two

Place on fold

Enlarge pattern 120%
for actual size

Dart

Trunk-style Body #3
You will need a front and back body pattern for this style body.

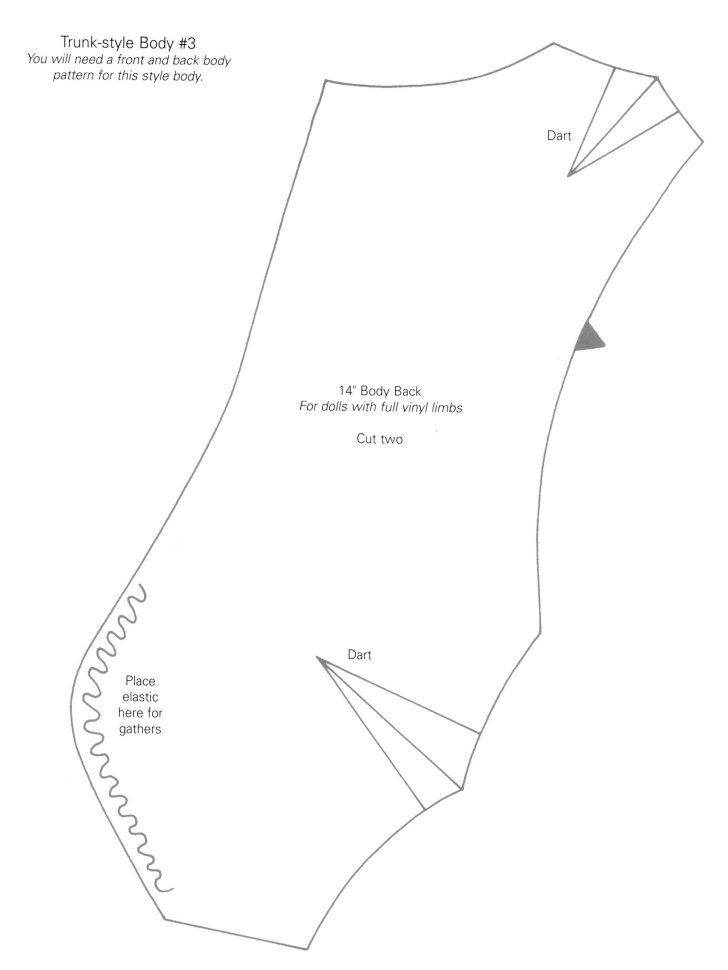

Dart

14" Body Back
For dolls with full vinyl limbs

Cut two

Dart

Place
elastic
here for
gathers

Trunk-style Body #3

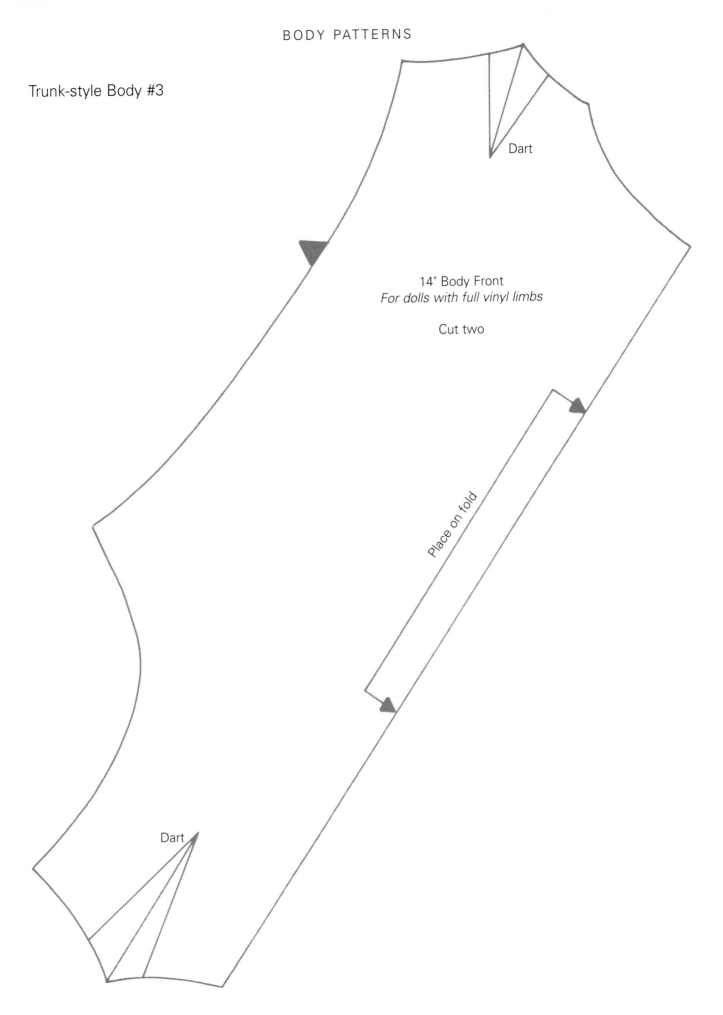

Dart

14" Body Front
For dolls with full vinyl limbs

Cut two

Place on fold

Dart

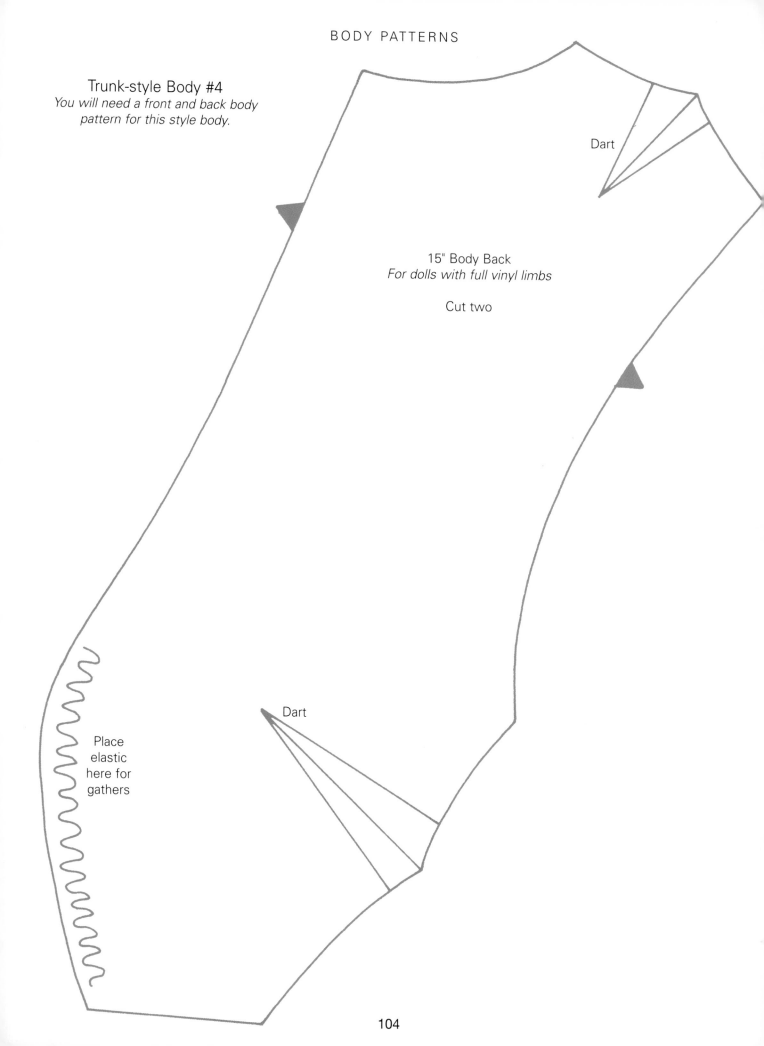

Trunk-style Body #4
You will need a front and back body pattern for this style body.

Dart

15" Body Back
For dolls with full vinyl limbs

Cut two

Dart

Place elastic here for gathers

Trunk-style Body #4

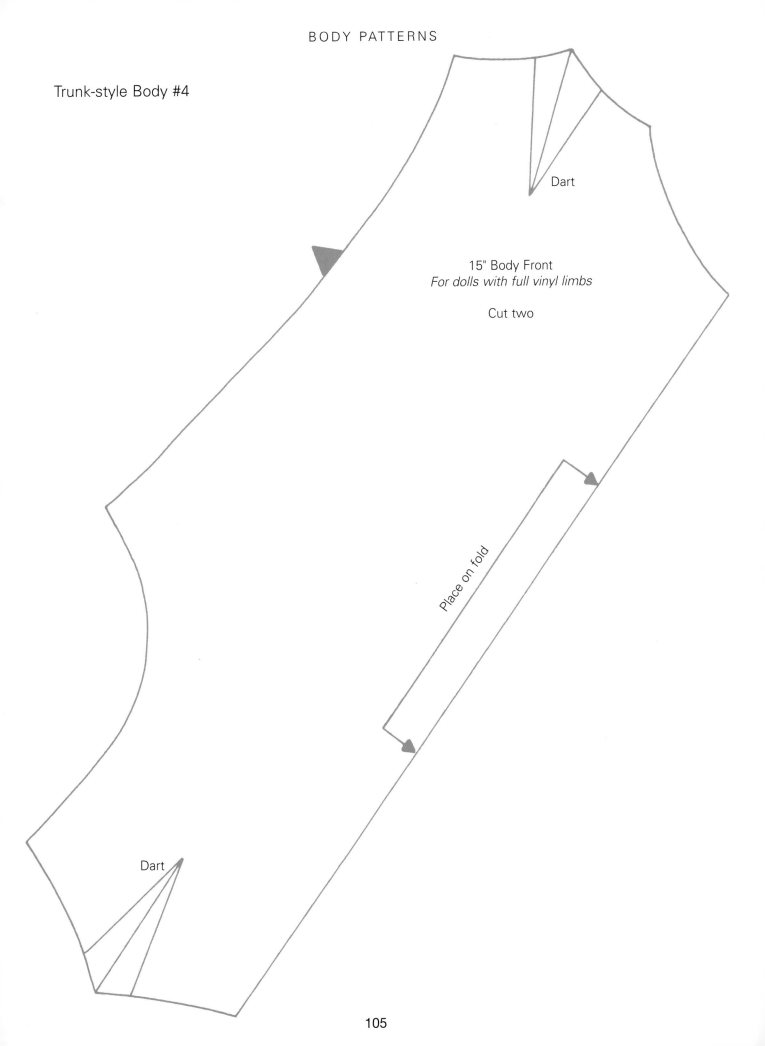

Dart

15" Body Front
For dolls with full vinyl limbs

Cut two

Place on fold

Dart

Trunk-style Body #5

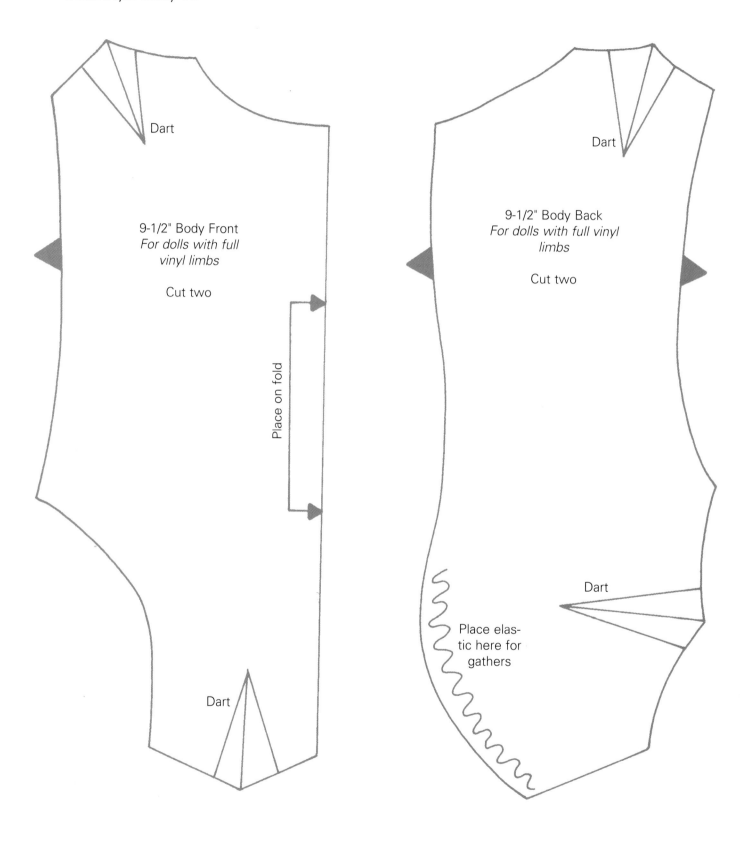

Dart

9-1/2" Body Front
For dolls with full vinyl limbs

Cut two

Place on fold

Dart

Dart

9-1/2" Body Back
For dolls with full vinyl limbs

Cut two

Dart

Place elastic here for gathers

Trunk-style Body #6

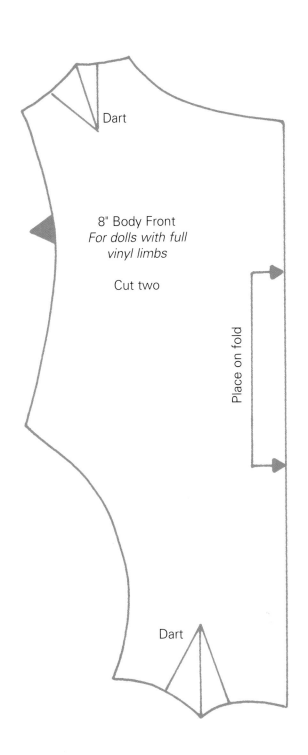

Dart

8" Body Front
*For dolls with full
vinyl limbs*

Cut two

Place on fold

Dart

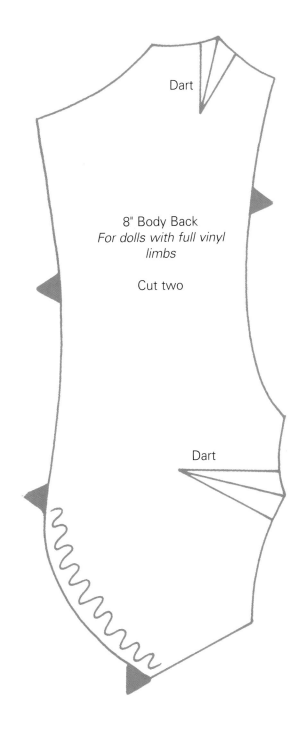

Dart

8" Body Back
*For dolls with full
vinyl limbs*

Cut two

Dart

Jointed, Partial
Limb-style Body #1
*You will need an arm, leg, and body pattern
for this style doll.*

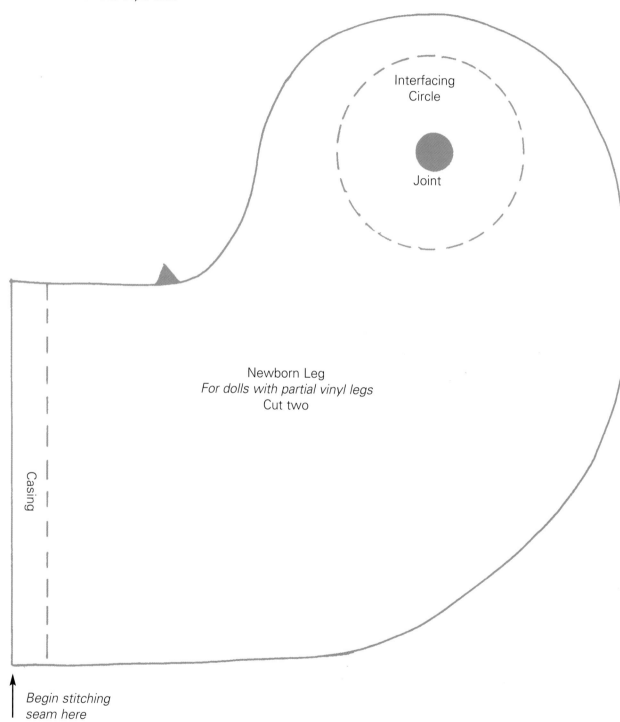

Interfacing
Circle

Joint

Newborn Leg
For dolls with partial vinyl legs
Cut two

Casing

*Begin stitching
seam here*

Jointed, Partial
Limb-style Body #1

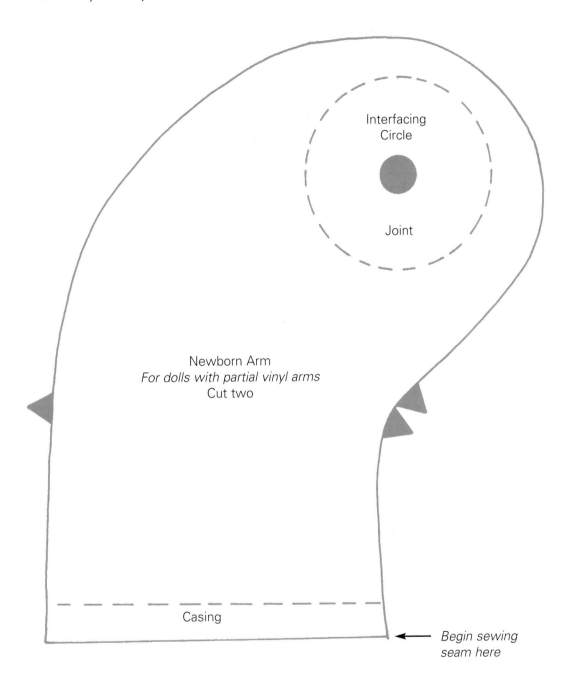

Interfacing
Circle

Joint

Newborn Arm
For dolls with partial vinyl arms
Cut two

Casing

← *Begin sewing
seam here*

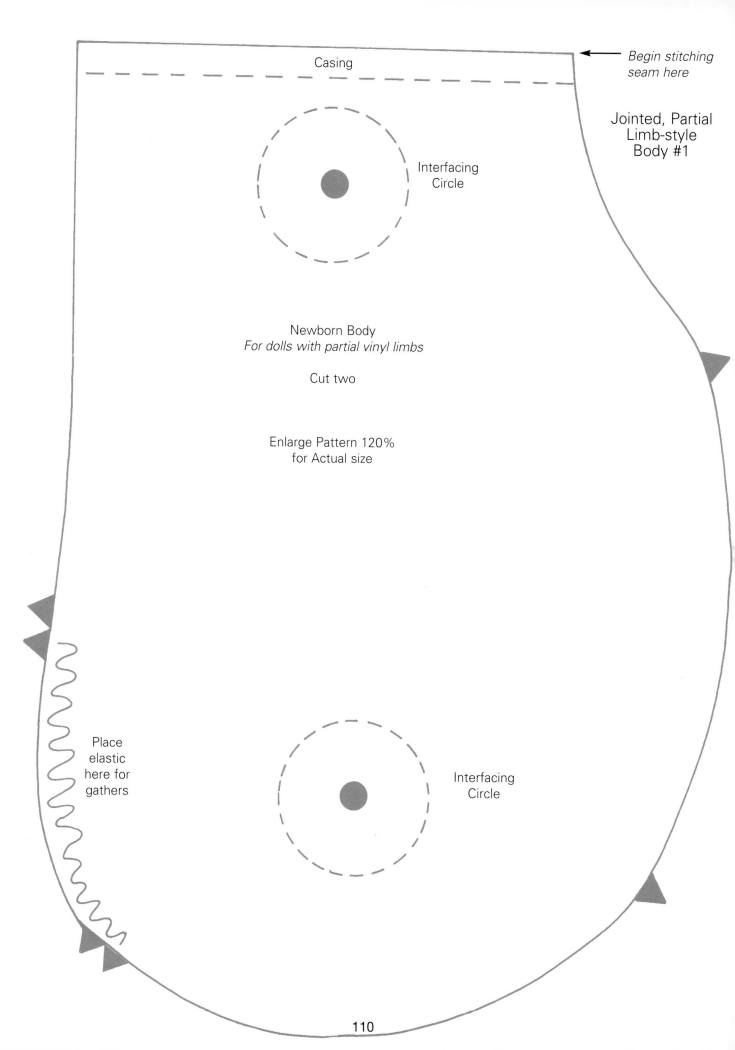

Casing

Begin stitching
seam here

Jointed, Partial
Limb-style
Body #1

Interfacing
Circle

Newborn Body
For dolls with partial vinyl limbs

Cut two

Enlarge Pattern 120%
for Actual size

Place
elastic
here for
gathers

Interfacing
Circle

110

Jointed, PartialLimb-style Body #2
You will need an arm, leg, and body pattern
for this size doll.

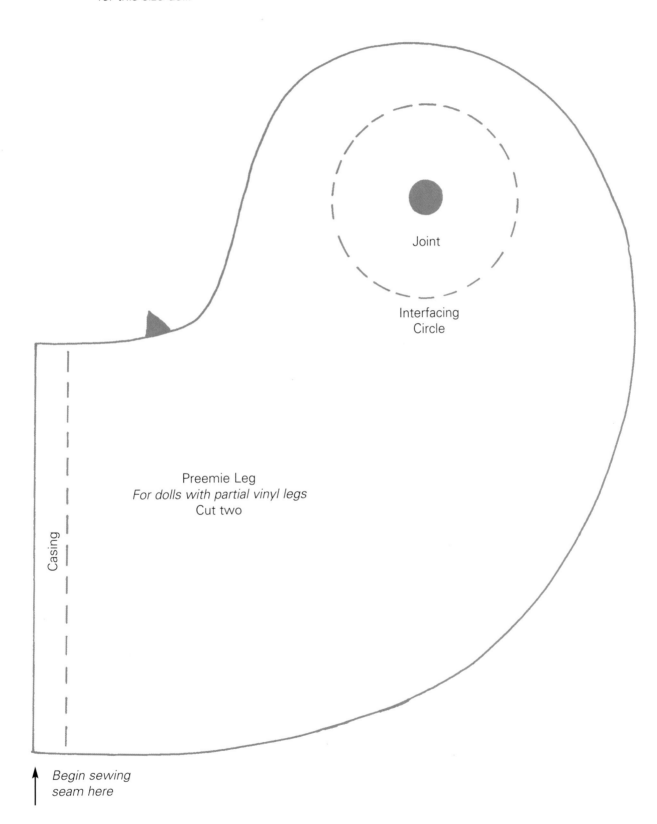

Joint

Interfacing
Circle

Preemie Leg
For dolls with partial vinyl legs
Cut two

Casing

Begin sewing
seam here

Jointed, PartialLimb-style Body #2

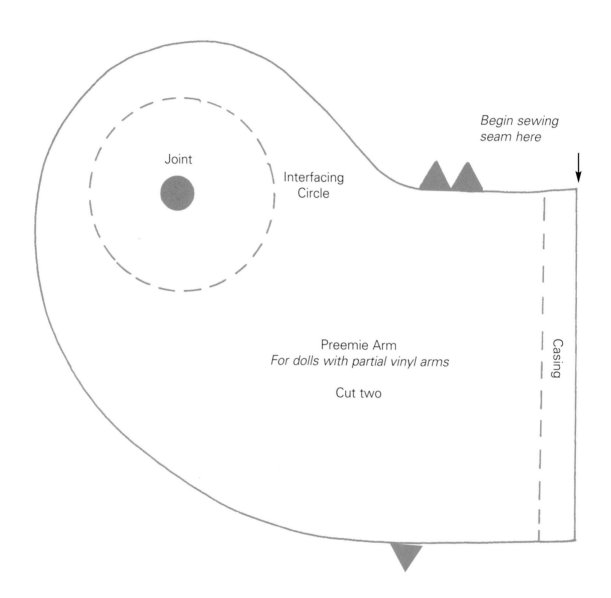

Joint

Interfacing
Circle

*Begin sewing
seam here*

Preemie Arm
For dolls with partial vinyl arms

Cut two

Casing

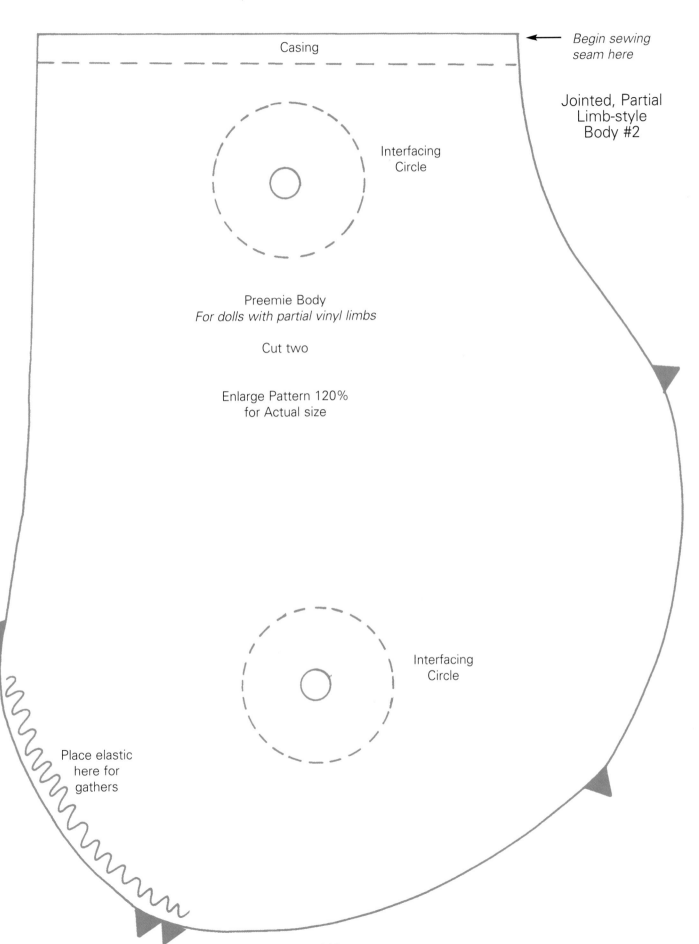

Casing

Begin sewing
seam here

Jointed, Partial
Limb-style
Body #2

Interfacing
Circle

Preemie Body
For dolls with partial vinyl limbs

Cut two

Enlarge Pattern 120%
for Actual size

Interfacing
Circle

Place elastic
here for
gathers

Gallery of Dolls

The dolls pictured in this section are the handiwork of my doll-designer friends. Aren't they amazing? Each has a personality of it's own, portraited by the doll artist.

Captured Moments Nursery

Hunny Buns

Hunny Buns

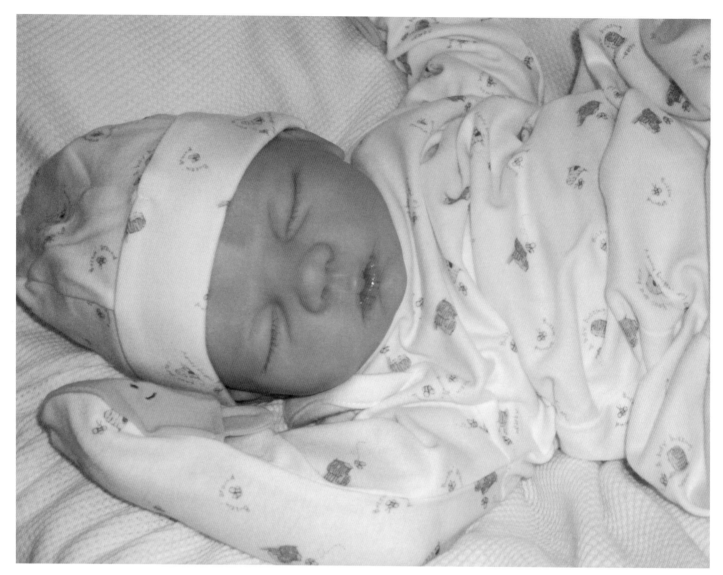

Captured Moments Nursery

Hunny Buns

Captured Moments Nursery

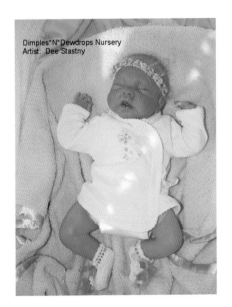

Captured Moments Nursery

Dimples 'N' Dewdrops

Little Lambs Nursery

Captured Moments Nursery

Captured Moments Nursery

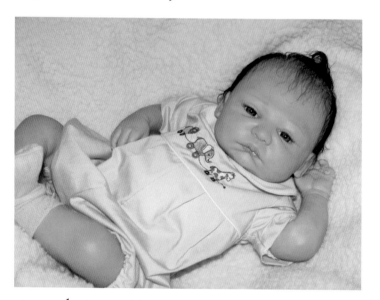

Captured Moments Nursery

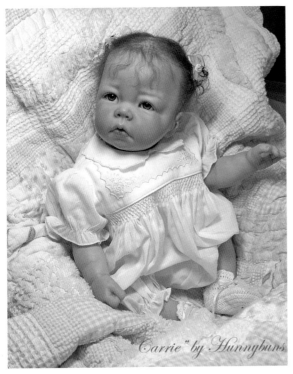

Carrie" by Hunnybuns

Hunny Buns

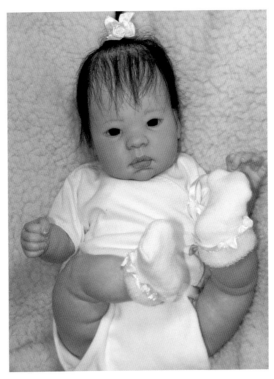

Captured Moments Nursery

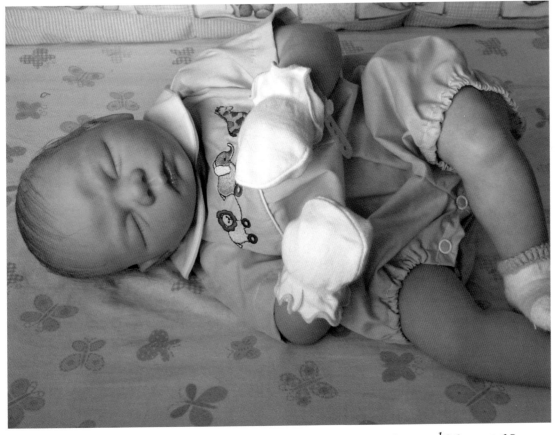

Captured Moments Nursery

Captured Moments Nursery

Captured Moments Nursery

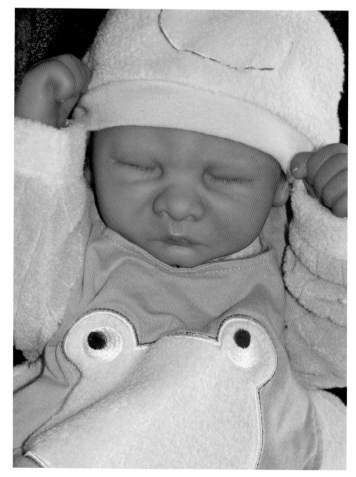

*Captured
Moments
Nursery*

Captured Moments Nursery

Little Lambs Nursery

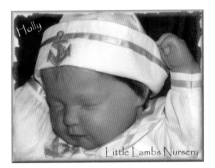

Hunny Buns

Hunny Buns

Olivia by HunnyBuns

Captured Moments Nursery

Captured Moments Nursery

Captured Moments Nursery

Hunny Buns

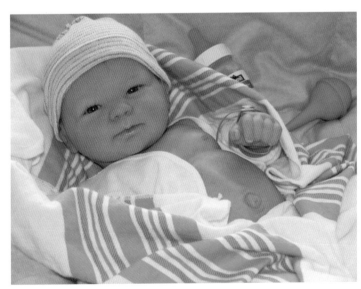

*Captured
Moments
Nursery*

beautiful Babys Nursery

Hunny Buns

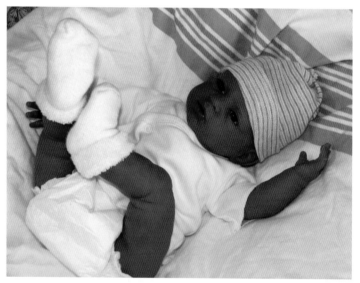

Captured Moments Nursery

Hunny Buns

Hunny Buns

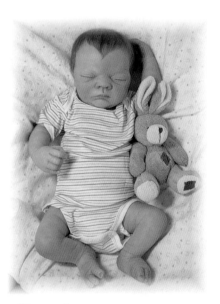

Hunny Buns

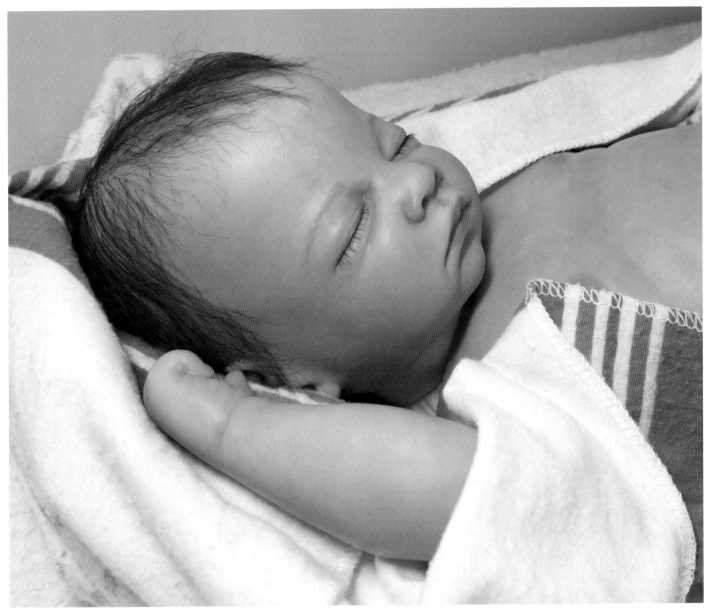

Captured Moments Nursery

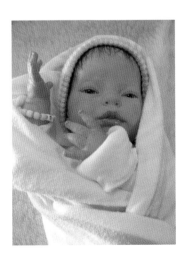

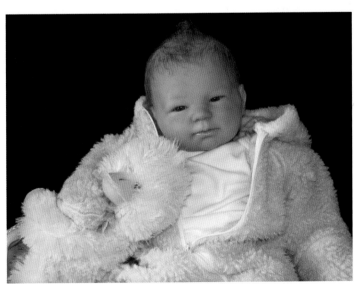

Captured Moments Nursery

Captured Moments Nursery

Metric Conversion Chart

Inches to Millimeters and Centimeters

Inches	MM	CM	Inches	MM	CM
1/8	3	.3	2	51	5.1
1/4	6	.6	3	76	7.6
3/8	10	1.0	4	102	10.2
1/2	13	1.3	5	127	12.7
5/8	16	1.6	6	152	15.2
3/4	19	1.9	7	178	17.8
7/8	22	2.2	8	203	20.3
1	25	2.5	9	229	22.9
1-1/4	32	3.2	10	254	25.4
1-1/2	38	3.8	11	279	27.9
1-3/4	44	4.4	12	305	30.5

Yards to Meters

Yards	Meters	Yards	Meters
1/8	.11	3	2.74
1/4	.23	4	3.66
3/8	.34	5	4.57
1/2	.46	6	5.49
5/8	.57	7	6.40
3/4	.69	8	7.32
7/8	.80	9	8.23
1	.91	10	9.14
2	1.83		

Index

Continued on next page

Index

L

Linseed oil 15, 25, 30

M

Magnet 12, 68, 69

Makeup sponges 14, 25, 29

Making Bodies 42

Marker 15, 30, 34, 46, 52

Measuring cup 14, 45

Metric Conversion Chart 126

Mohair 17, 34, 36, 37, 38, 72, 82, 87, 89, 96

N

Needles 17, 37

Newborn 10, 42, 43, 44, 45, 73, 74, 75, 78, 82, 85, 88, 89, 97, 100, 101, 102

Nose 40, 41, 76

O

Oil paint 15, 24, 25, 29, 30

Olivia 90

P

Pacifier 12, 52, 68, 69, 72

Paint 15

Paint marker 15, 31, 32

Paint remover 12, 13, 18, 23

Patterns 42, 43, 56, 58, 98-113

Payton Thomas 97

Permanent marker, see *Marker*

Plastic pellets 12, 13, 46, 47, 48, 49, 50, 52

Pliers 14, 37, 46, 49, 51, 52, 59

Polyester stuffing 12, 45, 46, 47, 48, 49, 52, 53, 56, 59

Preemie 42, 43, 44, 45, 72, 76, 77, 80, 81, 84, 87, 90, 91, 93, 96

Preparing the Doll 18

R

Ricci Sue 73

Rice 17, 37

Recoloring the Doll 24

Rooting needles 17, 36, 38

Rooting tool 17, 37, 38

Routing bit 14

Rubber gloves 14

Ryan Theodore 81

S

Sand 12, 46, 49

Sanding bit 14

Scissors 13, 14, 38, 46, 56, 63, 68

Scotty 84

Screwdriver 14, 18

Sewing machine 14, 46

Silicone 10, 72, 74, 82, 87

Silicone sealer 12, 13, 17, 38, 50, 51, 69

Sock 17, 25, 26, 37

Sponges 14, 25

Stencil brush 14, 29

Stencil paint 15, 27, 28, 30

Supplies for Making Doll Bodies 12

Suzanna 86

Sydney 87

Synthetic hair 17, 34, 36

T

Taylor Calvin 85

Thinning shears 17, 36

Thread 46, 56

Toddler 10, 83, 86

Tools 14

Toothpicks 14, 16, 23

Tracing paper 46, 56, 58

Tracing wheel 45, 56, 58

Transfer paper 46, 56, 58

Trunk style body 42, 43, 44, 45, 58, 59, 60, 92, 94, 96, 98, 99, 100, 101, 102, 103, 104, 105, 106, 107

U

Unjointed 42

V

Varnish 15, 16, 23, 31, 33, 39, 76

Vinyl 10, 11, 18, 19, 46, 50, 56, 65, 77, 80, 85, 90, 91, 93, 96

Viscose 36, 37

W

Watercolor pencil 15, 30

Weight bag 12, 42, 46, 48, 52

Wig 17, 34, 35, 36, 73, 75, 76, 78, 80, 83, 84, 85, 86, 90, 92, 94, 97

Wire cutters 14, 46, 50, 52, 59